# Norsk, Lapp and Finn

OR, TRAVEL TRACINGS FROM

## THE FAR NORTH OF EUROPE

BY

## FRANK VINCENT, Jr.

AUTHOR OF " THE LAND OF THE WHITE ELEPHANT," ' THROUGH AND
THROUGH THE TROPICS," ETC.

WITH ROUTE MAP AND FRONTISPIECE

LONDON
SAMPSON LOW, MARSTON, SEARLE & RIVINGTON
CROWN BUILDINGS, 188 FLEET STREET
1881

# PREFACE.

It was Goethe, if my memory serves me aright, who announced three test questions upon the correct answers to which the canons of literary criticism are based : first, what does the author propose to do ? second, is it worth the doing? third, has he done it well ? Since these searching interrogatories will doubtless be made in due course regarding the present writer, some explanation may be allowed him in reply to the first, the others being left to the consideration of notoriously impartial and cultured critics.

Though I have travelled much "up, down, and around the world," it has always been my aim to write only of the less-frequented and consequently the less-known countries, whether or not they offered the most romantic opportunities for picturesque description. In the present instance, fortunately, not only are the places and peoples I describe but little known, but the novelty also of customs and manners leaves me no excuse for being dull.

My prior wanderings were in the bright summerland of the Tropics, where, as Humboldt has happily remarked, "the native may behold all the vegetable forms

of the earth without quitting his own clime." Now
would I take my readers with me to the Arctic Zone,
the Tropics' natural counterpart. In this great division
of the earth, instead of large showy flowers and gigantic
parasitic plants, one finds the dwarf birch, the gray
alder shrub, pliant willows, and meads pale with lichen.
In zones where heat prevails, Nature pours out her
bounties so profusely that it would seem as though she
must perforce be niggard here. About the Equator I
found Man ardent and effusive, the emotions responding
with the vivacity of childhood to every impression,
whether sad or joyous; but north of the Polar Circle
his temperament becomes frigid and passive, and, as in
old age, almost insensible alike to pain or pleasure.
Could there be antitheses more striking? In such contrasts and comparisons, however, is found the greatest
charm of Boreal travel.

Scandinavia and Finland should be of additional
and special interest to us, since so many of their natives
emigrate to America, where, settling in the rural districts of the great Western States, they materially help
an agricultural development. Our manufacturing industries also are greatly benefited by the acquisition of
these skilful people of the North. Since 1820, 300,000
men and women have emigrated hither from Denmark,
Norway, Sweden, and Finland. Their children, born in
the United States, would about double this estimate,
thus raising the Norsk and Finn element in our population to a total of 600,000. The States selected as new
homes by these foreigners—who are still coming at the

rate of about 15,000 a year—stand thus in order of patronage: Minnesota, Illinois, Wisconsin, and Iowa. A small proportion of the emigrants are musicians, clergymen, and teachers; others are clerks or adroit artisans, such as carpenters, masons, and so forth. The vast majority are steady, frugal, hard-working laborers and farmers. A few are merchants, and many—of the women especially—are capable and faithful servants, and thus constitute phenomena unknown to New York and her surrounding cities.

Since the year 1556 there has been a small library of works published concerning these northern nations, though I have found no book which recognizes the ethnographical, philological, and topographical propriety of grouping all of them together for literary treatment. When thus combined they make the respectable showing of ten millions of people, occupying the entire northwestern corner of Europe—an area of nearly half a million square miles. It is natural that these enormous numbers should have given authors something to write about, but such books as still survive seem, for the most part, rather out of date or out of service, in that they do not show that contemporaneous *status* which, as supplementing the past, is essential to the student of civilization. It has, therefore, been my endeavor herein to present not only the latest, but also the most authentic information obtainable, together with such statistics, facts, and details as seemed necessary to furnish a clear idea of the intellectual, industrial, and commercial conditions of these countries, always bearing in mind that Man is vastly more important than Nature.

I have not forgotten that Bayard Taylor's Summer and Winter pictures of Scandinavia won the deserved reputation of being the best work in English in regard to this portion of the globe. It was written, however, a quarter of a century ago, and is, therefore, slightly antiquated. I fear that I am using this fact as an excuse for my own temerity, but I likewise remember that Mr. Taylor did not visit Finland at all, and that whatever personal knowledge he obtained of Denmark was acquired by a stay of three days only in Copenhagen, to a description of which he devotes less than two pages of his book.

One of the principal objects of my going abroad, however, was to study the Lapps as they were in their own homes and at their everyday labors and occasional recreations. This object I was able to accomplish entirely to my satisfaction so far as the gathering of the desired information was concerned ; but whether I have succeeded in transmitting my impressions in a desirable form to the public, is a question which I ask myself without being able to answer.

It is pleasant for the traveller who has told his tale to know that he has excited in the stay-at-home reader a curiosity to view for himself the distant landscapes of tenderness or grandeur and far-away people whose language, opinions, habits and institutions are vastly different from his own. The materials for creating this curiosity met me at every step during my journey

through the High North, and if the sequel proves that
I have failed to weave them into a volume having a
value more than fleeting, I shall have the sorrowful
conviction that I have fallen behindhand since my early
Oriental tours.

NEW YORK, *September*, 1881.

# CONTENTS.

## CHAPTER III.

### CHRONOLOGICAL COLLECTIONS.

## CHAPTER IV.

### THE METROPOLIS OF NORWAY.

## CHAPTER V.

### FIELD, FOSS, AND FIORD.

## CHAPTER VI.

### TWO OLD NORSE CITIES.

## CHAPTER VII.

### OFF AND ON THE COAST.

## CHAPTER X.

### COUNTRY, CHARACTER, AND CUSTOMS.

## CHAPTER XI.

### A DAY AT NORTH CAPE.

## CHAPTER XII.

### WITH THE LAPPS: BY THE SEA.

## CHAPTER XIII.

### WITH THE LAPPS. ON THE MOUNTAIN.

## CHAPTER XIV.

### THE REINDEER.

## CHAPTER XVII.

### An Excursion to the Copper and Iron Mines.

## CHAPTER XVIII.

### Upsala and Linnæus.

## CHAPTER XIX.

### Stockholm.

## CHAPTER XXII.

### KALEVALA, THE GREAT NATIONAL EPIC.

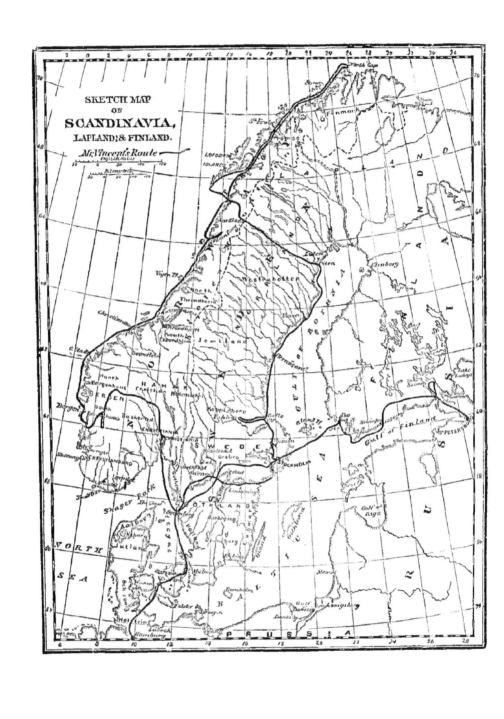

SKETCH MAP
OF
SCANDINAVIA,
LAPLAND & FINLAND.

Mr. Vincent's Route

# NORSK, LAPP, AND FINN.

## CHAPTER I.

### A Sea-Girt Kingdom.

HAVING left Paris by the afternoon express, the following noon you arrive in Hamburg. From this great bustling city of northern Germany, three routes lead to the capital of Denmark. The railway runs to the quaint old Hanseatic town of Lubeck, whence you may go by steamer to and across the Baltic, in about sixteen hours, directly to Copenhagen. Another course permits you to cover nearly the entire distance by land and by rail, passing northerly through the old Danish duchies of Holstein and Schleswig, then over a narrow belt of the sea—a mere ferry traversed in fifteen minutes,—to and through the island of Fyen, and thence by steamer in an hour-and-a-half, to Korsor, a town on the western coast of Sealand, and so on to the capital. This is a journey of twelve hours. The remaining communication is by rail to Kiel, thence to Korsor by steamer, and then by rail again to Copenhagen, requiring in all about fourteen hours.

The first mentioned route offers an opportunity to the traveller of visiting Lubeck with its decaying walls, its great gates, its proud towers, its spacious squares, its Gothic churches and gabled houses of red and black bricks, and its general mediæval aspect. The voyage by sea, however, is long and tedious. The second route is the shortest as regards time, the longest as regards distance. But the objects of interest are too many and too varied to be seen to advantage from a car-window; so constant a demand upon one's attention makes the journey tiresome despite the shortness of the time. The route which I have mentioned third in order is preferable, because it includes some glimpses of Holstein and a visit to the powerful naval station of Kiel in addition to the rail transit, with occasional stoppages, in the beautiful and interesting island of Sealand.

The reader is of course aware that Hamburg is the third grand commercial emporium of Europe, the first and second being London and Liverpool. It is also one of the great northern ports whence so many Germans leave their Fatherland in search of new homes in the New World. An interesting fact connected with this matter of German emigration has recently been made public by the Statistical Bureau at Berlin. The exodus from Hamburg during the first six months of the year 1880 was three times greater than in 1879, and four times greater than in 1878 or 1877. This enlarged emigration is attributed by the clerical press to religious persecution; the radical newspapers say it is

an unavoidable concomitant of political reaction ; while
the socialist journals are quite certain it is due to the
pressure of increased taxation and increased cost of
living. If to the latter explanation is added the extremely low scale of wages now prevailing there, we
shall probably arrive at the true cause of such an unpre-
cedented emigration from Germany.

The railway from Hamburg to Kiel passes through
an undulating country varied by pretty lakes, scanty
forests, turf-bogs and small cultivated tracts. There
are few villages and, with but two exceptions, these
are very small. Kiel, which is situated at the head of
a, long narrow bay of like name, possesses the finest
anchorage and the best winter harbor in the Baltic.
The water is so deep that the largest man-of-war may
approach without danger close to the shore. On these
accounts the Germans have selected it as the chief
station for their navy, and are erecting such invulner-
able fortifications that it will soon merit the title of the
Sevastopol of the Baltic. On the east bank of the
harbor are extensive dockyards, which may be viewed
upon application at the marine-office. The Germans
have also established here a capital training-school for
the education of youths who are intended for service
in the navy. Kiel itself is one of the oldest towns in
Holstein. Its present population is 38,000, which enu-
meration includes a large garrison. Beautiful walks
and drives abound in the environs.

In about an hour after leaving Kiel our little packet
steams out into the Baltic, gliding between formidable

batteries and fortresses on each side of the entrance
of the fiord. We are soon out of sight of land and in
a few hours more obtain our first view of Denmark,—
the fertile and wooded island called Langeland. This
contains three or four little towns, one of which is distinguished as being the birthplace of Œrsted, the discoverer of electro-magnetism and one of the greatest
physicists of modern times. We pass between this
island and the larger one of Fyen on the left, and then
cross an arm of the sea, called the Great Belt, to Korsor and Sealand.

The islands of Denmark are so crowded together as
almost to close the entrance to the Baltic. Their surface is uniformly low ; in this respect indeed they are
surpassed by but one country in Europe, namely Holland. The highest point in Denmark is only 550 feet
above the sea-level. Owing to these facts of position
and surface, it is subject, especially during the summer
months, to storms of wind and rain. The winters are
sometimes severe, though the climate might be regarded
on the whole as temperate. The scenery is of a quiet
and monotonous character, which charms by its grace,
but lacks power to inspire. The surface, which is generally fertile, is covered with meadows, cornfields, and
forests of beech. The largest province of Denmark,
however, the peninsula of Jutland, is for the most part
sandy and barren. More than half the country is cultivated or, to speak more accurately, is either in grass,
or lying fallow, or holds crops ripening for the harvest.
More than 2,500,000 acres are said to form a permanent

pasturage, and therefore, as might be expected, the work
of the dairy forms a very extensive branch of industry.

The name Denmark is supposed to have been de-
rived from the ancient Teutonic words dane or thane, a
prince or lord, and mark, a frontier country, thus corresponding in some degree to the German markgraf-
schaft, a frontier country confided to the protection of
an earl. This may be the correct etymology of the
word, for though Denmark has been an independent
kingdom more than a thousand years, it was at one
time subject to the dominion of the Goths. The people
were then divided into two classes, freemen and bonds-
men. The former busied themselves chiefly with war
and piracy; while to the latter were left the peaceful
pursuits of hunting, fishing, and tilling the soil. At the
present day the land is greatly subdivided, this being
encouraged by a law which interdicts the union of small
farms into large estates. About one-third of the nation
now live by agriculture. The island of Sealand has a
population of over 700,000; while that of the entire
kingdom of Denmark is nearly 2,000,000. Emigration,
averaging 3,000 persons annually, is considered at present rather slight, and is made chiefly to the United
States.

The first town of any importance after leaving Korsor is Soro, situated on a lake surrounded by beech and
pine woods. At a village near here a remarkable round
church nearly eight hundred years old is to be seen.
Its interior diameter is only thirty-four feet, and even
of this small space a considerable part is taken up by

four columns with bases of granite, each twelve feet in circumference and twenty-four feet high, supporting the roof, which at first was probably conical. This church is regarded as one of the most interesting monuments of ancient Christian architecture in Denmark. At the time of the planting of Christianity there its peculiar structure made it extremely useful as a fortified tower.

The next station, Ringsted, offering nothing worthy of attention, it is well to proceed to Roeskilde, whose sights are entitled to at least a day's inspection. This town, which is situated at the head of a long and narrow fiord, has 5,000 inhabitants. It is the second in point of population upon the island of Sealand, where there is but a single town of any very great importance, namely Copenhagen. The second city of Denmark is Odense, on the neighboring island of Fyen, with 15,000 inhabitants. Roeskilde was the capital of Denmark down to 1448 and once contained a population of 100,000. It was the residence of the bishop of Sealand until the Reformation, but since that epoch has fallen into decay, until now the sole relic of its ancient glory is the cathedral where repose the Danish kings from Harold to Frederick VII. The architectural merits of this diocesan church are not great. Notwithstanding that it is built of brick it has suffered considerably from fire, and in the various renewals. Its size has gradually been increased from century to century. One sees now pointed arches and round arches in juxtaposition; ancient towers and modern spires; an Elizabethan door and chapels of different styles. For some years, however, a thoroughly scientific and careful restoration has been in progress and in time this old cathedral may cease to shock the traveller by its conflicting anachronisms. The archbishop of the kingdom resides in Copenhagen.

Complete religious toleration obtains in Denmark. The state church is the Evangelical Lutheran. This also is the established religion of the other Scandinavian countries, as well as of Finland, notwithstanding the fact that the latter is a grand duchy of an empire which reckons 50,000,000 Greek Christians among its subjects. It is enacted by an article of the Danish constitution that "all citizens may worship God according to their own fashion, provided they do not offend morality or public order." No one can be deprived of his civil and political rights on the score of his religion, nor be exempted on that account from his duties as a citizen. Certificates of baptism and confirmation—and for the matter of that, of vaccination, too—are indispensable before entering into service, apprenticeship, or matrimony. Ninety-nine per cent of the population belong (nominally at least) to the Lutheran Church. For a long time the Mormons seemed to be making a special raid upon the Danish peasantry, but the emigration to Salt Lake City, I am pleased to be able to assert, is now but small. In Norway Mormonism is forbidden by the government, and no adherents to that creed and church are permitted to remain in the country.

From Roeskilde a short carriage excursion should
by all means be made to the little village of Om, where
a fine dolmen or burial grotto is to be seen.  Through
a passage twenty-two feet in length, formed by enormous stone slabs, I entered a sepulchral chamber
twenty-two feet long, six feet high, and eighteen feet
wide.  The farmer who was my guide said that when
this was opened, fifty years ago, it was found to contain
a number of skeletons and arms.  All parts of the
island of Sealand abound in these and similar vestiges
of antiquity.  North of Roeskilde, near a little town
called Fredericksvaerk, there is a great kjokken-mod-
ding, kitchen-midden or refuse-heap, in which relics
of the aboriginal inhabitants have been found.  The
place is of such importance and interest as to have
been visited by the International Archæological Congress, which was held in Copenhagen, in 1879.  The
whole neighborhood is rich in these dolmens, as well as
in barrows, tumuli, and raised stones with Runic inscriptions.

Denmark is especially the land of antiquities.  Sir
John Lubbock, in his work on " Prehistoric Times,"
maintains that the antiquity of Scandinavia is its most
splendid period, and is calculated to awaken even now
the greatest interest.  The monuments raised in prehistoric and earliest historic time of Denmark are very
numerous.  Under the thick layer of marsh-clay, peat-
bogs, and remains of ancient forests, discoveries have
been made of implements of flint, pottery, and other
relics of human civilization.  The study of these an-

tiquities has long been fashionable in Copenhagen. A society for the "preservation of antiquities" cares for those monuments which belong to the kingdom and a Royal Commission encourages, financially and in other ways, further explorations and disinterments.

There are also societies of a similar character in Germany, Norway, and Sweden. In their widespread enthusiasm for antiquarian science, the Germans are nobly led by their grand old emperor, who has lately defrayed from his own private purse the expenses of the excavations at Olympia, in Greece. Only a few months since some German archæologists found in what was a former province of Denmark (Schleswig-Holstein), a great lot of antique armor, huge and uncouth weapons of war, and mighty carved drinking horns. In Christiania, among many institutions for the promotion of science, art, and industry, an association flourishes for the preservation of Norwegian antiquities. This society was established nearly forty years ago with the avowed object of examining, preserving, and discovering Norwegian antiquities, and making them known to the world through the medium of pictorial representation and detailed accounts. Some members of this organization have recently made an archæological discovery of great import. In a mound on the shore of a bay named Sande fiord, on the southern coast, about twenty miles west of Christiania fiord, excavations have brought to light a boat some seventy feet in length. This is believed to be one of the fierce Vikings' ships, which were used for piratical expeditions upon the coasts of Britain and France, a thousand years ago.

A letter recently received from Norway, gives an interesting account of a visit to this venerable relic of the seas : " We reached Sande fiord at half-past one and drove immediately to the mound. All over Norway there are mounds which are known to be burial places. Now and then one is opened and the contents are always interesting, but it costs a great deal, so that it is only very gradually that these tombs are being investigated. This one is opened by the university at Christiania. When a famous chieftain died, it was the custom to build a burial chamber in his ship, and to bury with him his horses and dogs, the harness, gold and silver ornaments, etc. Then the ship was dragged up some distance on the shore, surrounded with moss, and buried in clay piled up over it. In the mound we saw there were found the ship, about seventy feet long (larger than any hitherto found), and the bones of a man, of three horses, and of several dogs. It was undoubtedly placed there in the ninth century, and after a thousand years of darkness has come to the light once more ; but not for the first time. There are signs of its having been opened and rifled of the gold and silver ornaments which ought to have been found and are not. But that was probably not long after it was first placed there.

" In spite of the years that it has lain buried, there are traces of paint on the outside, and its ornamentation convinces the antiquaries that some Viking of great

importance had his last resting-place here. The nails
with which the timbers are fastened show that it belonged to what is called the first iron age. It was curious
to see how some of the parts were dovetailed into each
other in just the same way as they would be done to-
day. The ship is supposed to have carried one hundred and twenty men, as that number of shields were
found hanging within the bulwarks, forming a defense
to the men who rowed beneath. The prow was very
sharp, and must have cut the water beautifully, urged
on by so many rowers, and also by the wind in its large
sail, which was of woolen material. Round the hero's
bones were found the remains of a silk mantle which
may have been brought from the farthest east. The
rudder, a huge oar-shaped thing, was fastened to the
vessel's side. Most of the articles found within the
ship have been carefully removed and placed in the
museum connected with the university. The ship is
not yet wholly excavated. If possible to remove it,
it will be taken to Christiania."

From Roeskilde to Copenhagen, about seventy
miles, the railway passes through a fertile and well-cul-
tivated country. When the traveller approaches the
capital he sees upon the right, the gardens and palace
of Fredericksburg; 'and upon the left, long rows of
workmen's houses and the general cemetery. Then the
train enters the thickly-built suburbs, and after crossing a long and narrow belt of lakes, halts at last in a
large and splendid station. The stranger jumps into a
droschky and is whirled across a bridge, through some

old fortifications, and along narrow and rough streets, until he reaches the *Hotel d'Angleterre*, a commodious and comfortable house situated on the Kongens Nytorv, the largest and handsomest square of the metropolis.

# CHAPTER II.

## THE MERCHANT'S HAVEN.

It is difficult, perhaps impossible, for a writer so to portray the general appearance and architectural characteristics of a large city, that they may afterwards be recognized by any one who visits it for the first time. The picture may therefore be thought nothing worth, when I say that standing, on a bright morning late in the June of 1878, on the summit of a lofty round tower in the heart of Copenhagen, I saw stretched below me a bewildering mass of red-tiled roofs, with pigeon-hole windows and brown chimney pots; an occasional bronze-plated steeple keeping watch, as it were, over a small green park, or broad paved avenue; a handsome distribution, as if at random, of universities, museums, hospitals, observatories, citadels, casinos, palaces, and custom-houses; dark woods and richly cultivated fields which presented the mediæval windmill in contrast to the modernism of the railroad; groups of fresh-water lakes, harbors filled with merchant ships and steamers; and finally the broad expanse of the azure sea, with a low range of coast line losing itself by imperceptible gradations upon the dim horizon.

The word Copenhagen is simply an anglicising of

the Danish Kjobenhavn, signifying the "merchant's
haven," and doubtless this city has been so named on
account of the perfect security its harbor offers for
trading vessels.   It is built upon the eastern and western coasts respectively of the islands of Sealand and
Amager, a narrow arm of the sea which separates them
forming its harbor.   The situation is so low that a
proper system of drainage has been almost impossible,
and I was not surprised to learn that the plague and the
cholera had been frequent guests.   The harbor is not
only safe but capacious, and is generally filled with
vessels engaged in loading the chief exports of the
country, such as corn, cattle, and dairy produce.   Ship-
building is in constant progress, and steamers of all
sizes continually come and go.   Indeed, there is
scarcely a seaport in Denmark between which and the
capital communication is not facile and frequent.   Toward the sea Copenhagen exhibits a long line of batteries and arsenals, docks, warehouses, and timber-yards.
Approaching it from the west, one must traverse the
straggling and lake-severed suburbs already mentioned.
Copenhagen would hardly be called a beautiful city.
The general quaintness of its architecture, the numerous canals penetrating to its very centre, and the varied
and picturesque spectacle offered by its markets,
wharves, and streets give it somewhat the appearance of
Amsterdam.   The modern buildings, however, interfere
with this effect and the boulevards, suggesting Paris,
are rapidly taking the place of the old fortifications,
which are being destroyed as past the age.

The city is not laid out at right angles, and though the streets are generally narrow and winding, they are for the most part kept scrupulously clean. Horse-cars and omnibuses run in every direction. Droschkies are numerous and a capital law for the comfort of the traveller forbids their drivers demanding a "pour-boire." Most of the stores are raised four or five steps from the sidewalk, which gives room for high basements beneath them, and has the additional advantage of placing their show-windows on a level with the eyes of the passer-by. It is an economical arrangement calculated to save rent for the seller and time and strength for the buyer. The large proportion of bookstores is noticeable. In the windows of the photographers, who largely abound, one is sure always to see displayed the pleasant face of Hans Christian Andersen, the genial author of the "Fairy Tales," and that of Thorwaldsen, Denmark's special pride, with pictures of his numerous famous sculptures. Danish specialties are the manufacture of articles in biscuit-china and terra-cotta. Their watches also are of rare excellence ; those of Jules Jurgensen, whose establishment I visited, having a world-wide celebrity. English is spoken in all the principal shops and hotels. Danish, however, is not a difficult tongue for English-speaking people to acquire owing to its peculiar affinity with their own language. The first-class hotels, cafés, and restaurants seemed to me quite equal to any others in Europe. The present population of Copenhagen is given at 250,000.

In the personal appearance of the Danes—their

yellowish hair, blue eyes, and square shoulders—and in their language, I was continually reminded of the Hanoverians.   But in their fashions, their houses, and habits, they recalled to me the French rather than the Germans.   Hospitality and affability appear to pervade all classes.   They are very fond of the theatre, of dancing, and of playing at cards.   Their gayety is quite surprising.   They possess nothing of the stolidity of the Dutch or the reserve and severity of the Norwegians.   They are fond of show and their nobility and the little court encourage this " small vice " as far as possible.   Clubs abound, and it is customary for a citizen to largely entertain his male guests at these, thus avoiding the expense and discomfort of home hospitalities.

The Danes are a refined and amiable people, carrying their politeness in some respects to an extreme. So frequently do the gentlemen bow to each other in the street that their hats seem to be more in their hands than on their heads.   It is considered the greatest breach of decorum to enter even the smallest shop without removing the hat.   In this respect they follow the custom of the Parisians and Viennese.   Even porters and hucksters salute one another with profound gravity. No place is deemed too public for such domestic pledges and confidences as we are accustomed to confine most scrupulously to our family circles.   Worse than this, the men there actually usurp the time-hallowed privileges of the women in matters of osculation ; for they hug and kiss each other on parting for a long absence or upon meeting afterwards, while the women, poor things, can only look sadly on at such times, taking no part in the conventional ceremonies through which Danish friendship and affection thus warmly express themselves. In Iceland, Denmark's best-known colony, the national salutation of welcome and farewell, is a kiss. But does not every country have its peculiar customs?

Elementary education is in Denmark widely diffused. It is rarely that you meet a person who cannot both read and write. This is doubtless owing to the fact that attendance at school is obligatory between the ages of seven and fourteen. In conformity with an article of the constitution, education is afforded gratuitously in the public schools to children whose parents cannot afford to pay for their teaching. With this sensible object in view nearly three thousand parochial schools are distributed over the kingdom. For the higher or classical training there is the University of Copenhagen and colleges in the principal towns, together with a large number of middle-schools for the children of the working classes.

With respect to institutions connected with education, science, and art, and especially those devoted to charitable purposes, Copenhagen ranks second to few, if any other cities in Europe. The University buildings occupy nearly the whole of a large square. Its library numbers some 250,000 volumes and its zoological museum is very rich and most admirably arranged. There are about fifty professors in the faculty, with an average attendance of a thousand students, about half of whom pursue theological subjects. The Astronomical Observatory contains one of the largest refracting telescopes in Europe. The Meteorological Institution publishes a daily weather map, and is in telegraphic communication with some twenty or more foreign stations. The Royal Library was founded about two hundred years ago. It contains at present over half a million volumes, with thirty thousand MSS., among which are some very scarce and valuable Scandinavian specimens. The publishers throughout the kingdom are obliged to send to this library, and also to that of the University, copies of all the books and periodicals published by them throughout the year. The first printing-press was set up in Copenhagen in 1490, eleven years after the University had been founded, and forty years after Gutenberg, at Mayence, had printed the quarto black-letter Bible now so exceedingly rare and precious. The first book published was a history of Denmark in rhymed verse. At present no censorship of the press exists, though of course authors and editors are subject to punishment for libelous, seditious, or morally pernicious publications, as in other countries where there is equal literary liberty.

Copenhagen contains a number of societies, the objects of which are sufficiently indicated by their names : such as the society for promoting Danish Literature, that for propagating the natural sciences, the geographical and agricultural societies, the Academy of Arts, etc. What is called the Royal Picture Gallery occupies the greater part of the upper story of an old palace. This collection consists of about a thousand paintings—Italian, Flemish, Dutch, and Danish. I could speak of the general high character of the latter, were it necessary at the present day to praise such artists as Marstrand, Exner, Hansen or Sonne, all of whom had works at the great Paris Exhibition of 1878.

Although Copenhagen possesses very many churches, two only are of special interest to the stranger—Vor Frue Kirke and Vor Frelser's Kirke. The former (Our Lady's Church) derives its chief renown from the sculptures of Thorwaldsen, by which it is decorated. In the tympanum of the Doric portico is his group representing John the Baptist preaching in the wilderness. Immediately upon entering the church, which is in the form of a Roman basilica, you see the splendid figure of Christ, and on each side of the nave the apostles. The frieze in the apse represents the procession to Golgotha. Over the entrance to the confessionals are two exquisite bassi-relievi, representing the Institution of the Sacraments. Vor Frelser's Kirke (Church of Our Redeemer), which is on the opposite side of the harbor, on the island of Amager, is quite an architectural curiosity. It has a very peculiar tower, nearly three hundred feet in height, on the outside of which a spiral staircase leads to the summit, where is a bronze ball capable of containing a dozen persons. Any one with a strong head who cared to mount three hundred and ninety-three steps, would be rewarded by a magnificent view of the Sound and surrounding coasts. This church is built in the form of a Maltese cross, two arms of which contain three tiers of boxes or enclosed pews, another holds the altar and a beautiful alabaster font, and in the remaining arm is a large organ in a splendid carved case which rests upon two enormous elephants. The latter are made of stucco and colored true to life.

I ought to mention here another curious spire which Copenhagen displays. It is that of the Exchange, a long narrow brick building grotesquely ornamented with gray sandstone in the Dutch renaissance style. From the centre rises, to the height of one hundred and fifty feet, a steeple which is formed of the entwined tails of four dragons, whose bodies and heads, forming the base of the spire, are turned to the four quarters of the globe. The architecture strongly reminded me of that of some portions of India.

The citizens of Copenhagen resemble the Viennese and Parisians, not only in the politeness of their manners, but also in their theatres, casinos, public balls, and parks and promenades. But the most popular resort of all is what is called the Summer Tivoli. This is a huge garden somewhat after the style of Cremorne in London, though frequented by much better company. It contains beautiful lakes, flower-beds, a labyrinth, a circus, a bazaar, an open-air theatre, a concert-hall with an orchestra of forty instruments, a panorama, a whirligig, and countless numbers of restaurants and beer-counters. Every few nights when these gardens are illuminated by thousands of colored lights and fireworks, six or eight thousand people meet and mix together there on the most friendly terms. On such occasions the quantity of bad tobacco smoked and of good beer drunk is something almost beyond conception. At any rate the sight is one not to be matched in any other capital in Europe. The general free-and-easy style is illustrated by the fact that the king and members of the royal family are frequently to be seen there strolling about with the most democratic air.

Should you inquire of a Dane what was best worth seeing in Copenhagen he would doubtless immediately direct you to Thorwaldsen's Museum. The name of this famous sculptor is mentioned everywhere in Denmark with the highest respect and veneration. Probably nowhere else in the world is there a museum devoted to the products of a single artist. Thorwaldsen, it may not be remembered by all my readers, was born in 1770 at Copenhagen. He was the son of a ship-carpenter from Iceland. At an early age he went to Rome and studied under the great Canova. It was long before his fame was established, but from that time until the close of his life, at seventy-two years of age, he basked in the sunshine of utmost prosperity. Most of his life was passed in Rome, and here it was he inaugurated a true revival of the masculine spirit of the ancients. Canova at once pronounced his Jason to be "a work in a new and grand style." Thorwaldsen only returned permanently to Copenhagen six years before his death, which occurred suddenly in March,

1842. The museum is erected in the style of the Pom-
peian and Etruscan tombs. Over the pediment of the
façade stands a bronze Victory reining in her quad-
riga. This sculpture is similar to the goddess en-
throned above the Brandenberg gate at the end of the
Linden, in Berlin. It was designed by Thorwaldsen
and was executed by his favorite pupil Bissen. The
remaining sides of the building are adorned with a
series of scenes in fresco—red, brown, and yellow colors
upon a background of black—representing the recep-
tion of the illustrious sculptor and his works at Copenhagen on his return from a residence of eighteen years
in Rome. This imposing structure, which contains
some three hundred pieces of his statuary—partly in
the original and partly in casts—is at the same time
his mausoleum, for he lies buried in the centre of the
court under a canopy of ivy. His works stand in mute
and marble admiration as though worshipping their dead
lord. Upon his return from Rome Thorwaldsen was
hailed by the Danes as the greatest master of modern
sculpture—a proud title which none since have successfully contested.

The principal royal residence, Amalienborg, is situated in the northern and aristocratic quarter of the city.
Here a large circle has been opened at the intersection
of two streets upon whose four corners stand palaces
which were originally built by rich noblemen in the
latter part of the past century. In the middle of the
open space inclosed by these edifices, which are plain
stuccoed affairs three or four stories in height, stands a

bronze equestrian statue of Frederick V. In one of the palaces dwells the King, in another the Crown Prince, in another the Queen Dowager, and the last is set apart for the service of the foreign office.

Christian IX., the reigning monarch, is about sixty years of age. He was crowned in 1863. His children have made the most brilliant matrimonial alliances of any dynasty of Europe. The heir-apparent, who is thirty-seven years old, is married to a daughter of King Charles XV. of Sweden and Norway. The eldest daughter, Princess Alexandra, is wedded to the Prince of Wales, heir-apparent of England. Prince Wilhelm, elected King of the Hellenes under the title of George I., selected as his Queen a Grand Duchess of Russia, daughter of one of the late Czar's brothers. The next child, Princess Dagmar, was espoused by Grand Duke Alexander, then Czarowitch but now Emperor of Russia; and another daughter became the bride of the late King of Hanover. The only child remaining is a young prince as yet unmarried—but who I trust may in due course have as good fortune as his noted brothers and sisters.

# CHAPTER III.

THE chiefest glory of Copenhagen, to my mind, is the Museum of Northern Antiquities and its proper supplement, the Chronological Collection of the Danish Kings. I can in justice compare the first to nothing in Europe, at least there is nothing with which I am acquainted so large and complete, nor so admirably arranged for purposes of study. To that extent are the Danes interested in the antiquities of their country, that the government promises the finder of any objects of precious metal their full value if they are offered to this museum. The second repository of chronological curiosities may be said to unite in itself the varied excellencies of the Imperial Treasury at Vienna, the Green Vaults at Dresden, the Hotel Cluny at Paris, and the South Kensington at London.

The collection of Northern Antiquities contains objects which are invaluable to the historian of early civilization. They consist of weapons, tools, implements, domestic utensils, hunting gear, wooden coffins, cinerary urns, musical instruments, trinkets, Runic inscriptions, ecclesiastical vessels, armor, tombstones, etc. There are about forty thousand specimens, all

arranged according to the order of time. Thus there
are five leading departments or periods represented—
the Flint, down to 1500 B. C.; the Bronze, to 250 A. D.;
the Iron, to 1000; the Mediæval Christian, to 1550;
and the Modern, down to about 1660. A learned and
most entertaining French catalogue, with capital illustrations, is furnished the visitor. The museum was
founded in 1807. The present director is Mr. J. J. A.
Worsaae, one of the most famous archæologists living.
He studied the general subject of Northern Antiquities
assiduously for several years and then travelled over
Europe, collecting everything which could serve to
throw light upon the early history and arts of the
Scandinavian peoples. He is the author of several
works, in Danish and in English, of the highest antiquarian value.

The collection of which I have been speaking is
displayed in twenty rooms, the first eight of which are
the most interesting. The others contain objects which
may be matched in several other museums. In the
first room one sees sections of the celebrated kitchen-
middens, which have been discovered at more than fifty
points along the shores of Denmark. These consist of
oyster-shells, indicative of the staple food of the ancient
inhabitants of the country, and pieces of rude pottery
and domestic implements of stone and bone found em-
bedded in them. The second and third rooms contain
a great variety of stone axes, arrow-heads, and knives,
many of them beautifully ground and polished. The
fourth and fifth rooms are devoted to bronze tools and

arms. Here are some coffins hollowed out entire from trunks of oak trees, and containing garmented bodies the oldest known. One notices also many gold ornaments. The remaining rooms are occupied by relics of the middle ages, running through the period of the renaissance down to 1660. The time extending from that year to the present day is illustrated by the chronological collection of the kings of Denmark.

The Ethnographical Museum in the same building is also one of the most extensive in Europe, occupying, as it does, twenty-eight rooms. It is roughly divided into two grand departments : Ancient Times and Modern Times. The former comprises antiquities of nearly all the world save the north of Europe; and the latter division embraces objects from primitive and barbarous non-European nations, illustrative of their arts. The catalogue here is in Danish, which, from the strong resemblance to English I have remarked, is of considerable assistance in studying the contents of the respective rooms.

One is much struck by the paleolithic implements and specimens of the rude attempts at art by primeval man — the "man of the cavern" — contained in this splendid museum. They resemble in many important respects those now in use among the Esquimaux. And it is interesting to note that quite recently Prof. Boyd Dawkins, of England, has expressed his belief that from their mode of living and especially their not caring to bury their dead, the cave men were indeed a sort of Esquimaux, and that the latter people of the present day represent the cave men as they lived in Europe during ages long gone by.

The collection of the kings of Denmark is preserved in the palace of Rosenborg. The design of this building, probably the most picturesque in Copenhagen, has been attributed to the genius of the celebrated architect Inigo Jones. It is entirely devoted to this museum and one or more rooms are dedicated to the reign of each Danish king, being decorated in the style of the period and filled with contemporaneous furniture, arms, ceramics, jewels, medallions, coins, dresses, pictures and miscellaneous objects of art. The historical arrangement of this collection is probably not excelled by that of any other. It also is under the management of Mr. Worsaae, who has classified it under three grand periods of Danish history, covering about four hundred and thirty-three years, as follows: (1) 1448—1648, before and under Christian IV (Renaissance); (2) 1648—1808, Christian IV. to the French Revolution (Rococo style); (3) 1808—1881, French Revolution to our own Times (Imperial Renaissance). It requires half a day to gain a general idea of their contents by merely walking through the rooms. I have not a tenth part of the necessary space to properly describe the most remarkable objects—the ancient drinking-horns, the jewelled orders, the silver and gold-hilted swords, the tables, the candelabra, the jewel-boxes, crystal and gold goblets, falcon-heads, vases, cabinets, clocks, coronation-chairs, etc., etc.

I must, however, briefly refer to a few famous

curiosities. First perhaps stands what is called the Oldenborg horn, which dates from the fifteenth century. It is of silver, richly gilt and enameled and decorated over the entire surface, partly with engraved figures of dragons and serpents, and partly with embossed ornaments of coats-of-arms and inscriptions. The general character of the ornamentation is an inspiration of the middle ages. The whole has evidently been intended to represent a walled town, the spires of which form the lid and knob in which the points of the horn terminate ; while the entrance is beneath two towers by which it is supported. There are also to be seen balconies, ladies playing on the lute, knights and esquires. In short a picture in miniature of the life of chivalry is depicted in its many colored diversity. Upon the knob sits a little savage holding a narrow scroll, with an inscription signifying, "Empty the horn !"

In the room devoted to the times of Christian IV., the middle of the eighteenth century, there is a splendid vase nearly four feet in height upon which a famous artificer of that period, named Magnus Berg, is said to have labored for twelve years. It is composed chiefly of gold, silver, and ivory. On the top, above a crystal dome, a swan swims in a mussel-shell. Under what may be styled the cupola there is a splendid carving of the expedition of Galatea over the sea. Upon the surface of the principal piece are cut, in bas-relief, figures of Neptune, Polyphemus, Europa, and Acis. The handles and exterior supports are formed of dolphins, nereids, and tritons. The pedestal consists of

four dolphins, which from each corner spout water into
a mussel-shell. These dolphins, as well as the nereids
and tritons, are fashioned of silver and ivory alternately.
The middle part of this wondrous vase is of ivory,
bound above and beneath by richly gilded, chased and
embossed silver-work; the band also which runs over
the crystal dome to support the swan, is of silver and
gold in the form of fruits and leaves. Altogether this
fabric is a marvellous exhibition of skilful and patient
labor.

The third floor of the palace of Rosenborg is entirely taken up by a great banqueting-hall. Upon the
walls, which are hung with rare and valuable tapestries,
are many fine paintings, and the vaulted ceiling is covered with beautiful stucco reliefs. In the centre is the
Danish escutcheon with its proper heraldic colors, while
about it are the emblems of royalty—four large paintings. At one end of this hall stand two very curious
old coronation-chairs. The larger is about eight feet in
height and made almost entirely of narwhal horn, which
material, two hundred years ago, was worth its weight
in silver. It is ornamented by eight allegorical figures
formed of gilded metal, of which four sit on the exterior
near the arms, two in recesses above the back, and two
in recumbent positions upon the canopy, whose apex
terminates in the globe and cross. In a hollow space
beneath this is a large piece of crystal-spar, which on
the day of coronation is replaced by an amethyst, said
to be the finest in existence and at present preserved
among the Regalia. The canopy is still further decora-

ted by two enormous oval moss-agates, the gift of an
Indian prince.    The seat, back, and arms are covered
with gold brocade.

I made several visits to both these grand Danish
museums, and finally concluded that weeks of examination given to them would not be ill-spent.    But,
since so much time for such a purpose was not at my
disposal, I beg the reader to accompany me in bidding
farewell to these innumerable traces of the great ages
of stone, bronze, and iron down to and including
those of printing and steam, and to consider a few of
the more obvious outgrowths of the age of peace —
commerce, culture and colonization.

The vessels annually entering Copenhagen number
more than ten thousand.    The exports of Denmark
consist almost entirely of agricultural produce, such
as corn, barley and butter, and live animals—oxen,
sheep and horses, together with leather, wool and train-
oil.    The finest cavalry horses used in the German
army come from this little kingdom.    In 1877, the
total exports, half of which were to Great Britain and
Germany, amounted to about $45,000,000.    The prin-
cipal imports are cotton manufactures, coal and iron.
During the same year the value of these, coming chiefly
from Great Britain and Germany, was over $60,000,000.
Formerly protective duties of a most unjust and unwise
character were enforced in Denmark.    The commercial
legislation was even restrictive to such a degree that
imported manufactures had to be delivered to the customs, where they were sold by public auction, and the

proceeds of this the importer received from the custom-houses after a deduction was made for the duty.

The Danes though few in number yield to no people in Europe in industry and enterprise. The king sets the example in his devotion to the development of the interior resources and the popular institutions. Though little room for railway is apparent, yet nearly a thousand miles of it exist. About two-thirds of this belong to the State. There are also telegraph lines to the linear extent of 2,000 miles, and submarine cables are laid to England, Norway, Sweden and Russia. The public debt of Denmark, which now amounts to about $50,000,000, has been almost wholly incurred in improvements of a very useful and important character, such as the construction of railways, harbors and light-houses, and the founding of schools and museums. Even this comparatively small indebtedness — small for a modern European nation — is being rapidly reduced.

The colonies of Denmark are all islands—if as Dr. Hayes, the Arctic explorer, seems to think, Greenland may be ranked as such. The others are Iceland, the Faroe group, and the three islands of St. Croix, St. Thomas, and St. Johns in the Lesser Antilles. These colonies aggregate about six times the area of Denmark proper — which is even a smaller country than Switzerland — though they have a population only one-tenth as great. Iceland, which is exactly the same size as our State of Virginia, is a mountainous island, the greater part of whose surface is a dreary wilderness of lava. It contains 75,000 people, who are mainly engaged in

fishing and cattle-raising. Greenland is nearly as large
as Germany and France taken together. Its population however is less than 9,000, of whom only 300 are
Danes. The country is mountainous and barren, and
covered with glaciers. These two islands constitute
what is known as Danish America. The Faroe islands,
containing a population of about 10,000, lie nearly
midway between the Shetlands (about 150 miles northeast of Scotland) and Iceland. They export to
the Danish markets tallow, sheep-skins, feathers, and
train-oil.

But of all the colonies of Denmark, those in the
West Indies are alone of any great commercial importance. Unitedly these have about 40,000 inhabitants.
St. Croix is much the largest, with a population—
mostly free negroes—of 25,000. The cultivation of the
sugar cane is the chief industry. About fifteen million
pounds of raw sugar, and a million gallons of rum are
annually exported. The imports are mainly cotton
goods. A few years ago St. Thomas was offered for
sale to the United States government, which came very
near purchasing it, but for some good reason doubtless
the negotiations were suddenly broken off.

The chief interest of European Denmark seems to
centre in Copenhagen, though some of her colonies
still present broad fields of interesting travel and research. How inviting, for instance, is Greenland in its
connection with Polar exploration and its still unknown
northern boundary. Then there is Iceland, land of
prodigies, with its glaciers and hot springs, its volcanoes

and mountain plateaus, its beautiful caverns and gaunt deserts, which Baudelaire might have loved to dream about. Its historical and political interest also is very great. I need but refer to the carefully preserved Icelandic Sagas which prove that America was discovered in A. D. 986, more than five hundred years before the reputed discovery by Columbus; and to the constitution, restoring the self-government of the island, which King Christian granted the people on the occasion of his visit, in 1874, to the millennial festival commemorating its first colonization.

Steamers from Copenhagen to Reikiavik, the capital of Iceland, now run regularly every month, calling at Aberdeen in Scotland and at the Orkney, Shetland and Faroe islands. The distance is something like 1,500 miles; the voyage by steamer, with customary stoppages, employs a week, or by sailing vessels direct, about two weeks.

## CHAPTER IV.

### The Metropolis of Norway.

SEVENTY-FOUR hours are required to cover the distance between Copenhagen and Christiania. The service is performed by a very comfortable and fast line of steamers which sail three times a week from Copenhagen, making a brief stay at Gothenburg, in Sweden, whence the traveller may go, in twelve hours by rail, direct to Stockholm.

We kept close along the coast of Sealand which was very picturesque with its rich cornfields, green pastures and fine beech forests, enlivened with numerous chateaux, farm-houses and villages. At Elsinore the Sound, which at Copenhagen is about twenty miles in breadth, had narrowed to a trifle over two miles. Upon the opposite bank, in Sweden, was the old seaport town of Helsingborg. The channel between it and Elsinore might be termed the gate of the Baltic, for here one is certain always to see going in or out hundreds of ships and steamers. Formerly all vessels passing here were subject to a toll, for the Danish Crown looked upon the Sound as exclusively her property since she at that time possessed both sides of its entrance. For over a century this right was never successfully contested by the other powers, though the regulations made from time to time concerning the tax at last led to hostilities between Denmark, and Sweden and Holland. The United States, however, was the first to declare its purpose to submit no longer to the old usage. The obnoxious duties were therefore entirely abolished, in 1857, in consideration of an award to Denmark of $17,500,000 by the nations most interested in the commerce of the Baltic.

We pass near the Kronborg, a picturesque fortress of a quadrangular form rising conspicuously beyond the town. It was built over three hundred years ago, but of course has since been added to and repaired so much as to be almost another structure. One of the ramparts called the Flag Battery is said to be " the platform of the castle of Elsinore" where the ghost appeared to Hamlet. The scene of another popular legend is also laid here. The tutelary genius of the kingdom, Holger Danske, familiar to all readers of Andersen's fables, is said to repose beneath the old citadel, ready to arise when Denmark is in danger. While speaking of legends, I may as well say that this is not the Kronborg of Shakespeare and of Hamlet, for the melancholy prince lived in a different part of the country, and a thousand years before Kronborg was built.

Leaving Elsinore, which is a very old town of about 9,000 inhabitants, we passed out from the sparkling blue Sound into the dark green waters of the Kattegat, "strait of Catti," the Catti being a nation anciently dwelling in the northwestern part of Europe. The

strait is nearly 100 miles in width and perhaps 150 in
length. It contains a few small islands, and many
sandbanks dangerous to navigation. We stopped at
Gothenburg in Sweden, and nearly opposite the Skaw
or extreme northern point of Jutland. Of this Swedish city, where our steamer stayed only twenty minutes,
I shall have something to say further on. We next
entered that broad arm of the North Sea known as the
Skager Rak, the "crooked strait of Skager," which
though of about the same dimensions as the Kattegat
is much deeper. Frequently violent storms visit this
strait, but we were favored with most delightful weather.

Early on the following morning we entered the fiord
or bay of Christiania fifteen miles in width at its mouth,
at the northern extremity of which, some seventy miles
distant, is situated the metropolis of Norway. The
fiord is classed among the select portions of Norwegian scenery. Its beauty however is of a very mild type.
The low banks are covered with fir and pine trees and
in parts the glossy expanse is studded with diminutive islands. In a particularly narrow reach is built a
strong fort. Soon villas appear, afterwards glimpses of
churches, then the new palace and the castle of Agershuus, and now, rounding a small island, the entire city
is distinctly seen upon the sloping sides of a chain of
low hills running east and west. We slowly enter the
harbor and gliding by a few vessels, drop anchor opposite the custom-house. A hurried and partial examination of baggage and I am on the shore of the great
peninsula of Northern Europe. I walk up a clean

broad street which is lined with low houses, pass a large
church, then the Post-office, then the Parliament-house
and at last reach the Grand Hotel, which is to be my
temporary terminus.

Christiania derives its name from King Christian IV.
by whom it was founded about 250 years ago. It is laid
out in rectangular blocks, with large squares, market-
places and public gardens. Its present population is
nearly 120,000. There is not however, much of interest
to be seen here. Christiania is rather a large town,—a
great assemblage of dwelling-houses and stores, and possesses very few of the attractions we are accustomed to
associate with the word city. The public buildings are
few in number and not imposing in appearance. There
is but one theatre and but one music-hall. The long
narrow streets seem almost deserted. At one end of
that on which my hotel was situated stands the royal
abode, a huge quadrangular brick edifice painted yellow and much more resembling a factory than a king's
palace.

The day following my advent, the king arrived from
Stockhólm on a visit to his Norwegian subjects. H.
M.'s civil list as King of Norway is about $150,000 a
year, and he is accustomed to pass some weeks every
summer in Christiania. He rode from the railway station to the yellow factory above mentioned in a barouche
drawn by four horses, followed by his suite in other car-
riages, and escorted by a troop of cavalry and a band of
music. The present king was crowned in 1872. He is
the grandson of Bernadotte, Napoleon's famous marshal,

who, as the reader is aware, ascended the throne of the Swedes under the name of Carl Johan XIV. Before his accession he was general of the army. He is a tall, slender man of soldierly bearing, with a large well-shaped head, and an expression whose frankness and pertinacity are not concealed by a full beard. He appears to be about fifty years of age. His abilities and acquirements are far beyond the average of crowned heads. Besides the duties imposed upon him by his lofty position, he has given much time to literature and authorship. His poetical translation of Goethe's " Faust " into Swedish was of sufficient merit (considering his kingship), to procure for him from the Frankfort Academy of Sciences, an election as corresponding member. The king is also in the habit of frequently contributing articles to the Stockholm magazines and newspapers, and would make an excellent "special " for the New York press. His last published volume is entitled " Poems and Leaflets from my Journal."

The castle of Agershuus commands the entrance to the harbor. A part of it was built upwards of five hundred years ago, but it is not of any special military importance at the present day. It contains the Regalia of Norway, the national records, and a small collection of old armor. Here also in a room or cage formed of thick iron bars, was immured for life a most notorious criminal named Hoyland, who is entitled to figure as the Robin Hood of Norway. A recent writer says " his vices were inordinate love of the fair sex and theft. He was a native of Christiansand, where he began his career. On being imprisoned for some petty theft, he broke into the inspector's room while he was at church, and stole his clothes ; in these Hoyland dressed himself, and quietly walked out of the town unobserved and unsuspected. He was afterwards repeatedly captured and imprisoned in the castle, and as often made his escape. Previous to his last evasion, all descriptions of irons having been found useless, he was placed in solitary confinement in the strongest part of the basement of the citadel. Here he had been confined for several years when one day his cell was found empty and the prisoner gone, apparently without leaving a trace of the manner in which he had effected his flight. On removing his bed it was found that he had cut through the thick planks of the flooring, which he had replaced on leaving the cell, and had sunk a shaft under the wall of his prison which enabled him to gain the courtyard and reach the ramparts unseen. About twelve months afterwards the National Bank was robbed of 60,000 rix dollars, chiefly paper money, and in the most mysterious manner, there being no trace of violence upon the locks of the iron chest in which the money had been left, nor upon those of the doors of the bank. Some time afterwards a petty theft was committed by a man who was taken, and soon recognized to be Hoyland. At last he hanged himself in prison in despair."

The object of most travellers in visiting Norway seems to be to obtain a sight of the midnight sun, which perhaps Mr. Barnum, with his happy phraseology, might call the "biggest show on earth." For this pur-

pose they voyage up the western coast as far as Tromsoe
or Hammerfest or the North Cape, according to the season of the year. Nearly two thousand miles of coast
from Christiania, the capital, to Vadso, in Finmark,
are thus connected by means of comfortable mail
steamers. But one who makes this journey only misses
some of the finest scenery in Norway and fails also to
make acquaintance with an interesting people. There
are three routes overland from Christiania to the west
coast, each of which boasts of some special attractions
for the stranger. The best is without doubt that over
the Fille Field. This route—leading from Christiania
to the head of the Sogne fiord, thence across to the
Hardanger fiord, and thence to the city of Bergen—
presents a series of valleys, mountains, bays, glaciers,
waterfalls and islands unequalled for grandeur and
beauty anywhere else in Scandinavia.

The principal fiords, as well as the entire seacoast,
are navigated by good steamers. There is a railway
from Christiania to Trondjhem, about three hundred and
fifty miles, with some lake connections, and a few other
short lines in the immediate neighborhood of the metropolis. The only popular and comfortable manner of
traversing the hilly interior is by means of that curious
vehicle called the carriole. This is a species of gig
somewhat resembling the Italian carricola, with large
wheels and long elastic shafts fastened directly to the
axle. The seat, which is long and narrow, like a scallop-
shell, and of sufficient size for one person only, rests by
cross-bars upon the shafts. You sit with legs extended

almost horizontally, the feet bracing against one of the cross-bars and shafts, as in a skeleton sulky, to prevent the possibility of being thrown out, since many of the roads are quite steep and rough. Your trunk or other luggage and a bag of hay for the horse, are carried behind the axle-tree upon a board attached to the ends of the shafts. Here also sits the postilion, a boy— sometimes it is a girl !—who is to take back the horse at the end of the stage, the traveler generally driving himself. The horses are attached to the carrioles by the minimum of harness. The shafts simply rest upon an iron back-yoke fastened by a short strap with a wooden peg ; there are no traces. The horses, many of them no larger than those of the well-known Shetland breed, are very docile and capable of great exertion. They are driven without the whip, the Norwegian driver employing a peculiar sibilant sound for increasing their speed, and a sort of burring noise when desiring to stop them.

As a rule the roads are remarkably good, being macadamized and kept in order by the landed proprietors. There are no toll-bars, but an annual tax is paid for every horse. The sled or sleigh drawn by reindeer, called a pulkha, and employed for winter travel in Lapland, resembles somewhat the carriole without its wheels.

Carriole traveling is carried on by posting under government control, there being fixed stages, with station-houses varying from seven to ten miles apart. The charges, the equivalent of about fifty cents a Norsk

mile (seven English), are regulated by law.    Formerly
it was necessary in posting to send forward, either by
messenger or post, an order for horses at each station
where they would be wanted, stating the day and time
of the traveler's expected arrival.    This was termed
sending forbud.    But now on all the principal roads the
postmaster is obliged to keep a certain number of horses
and carrioles in readiness and it is only in the very
remote districts that the forbud is in use.    These two
species of station are called, the one a "fast," the other
a "slow" station.    At the latter the farmers in the district are in turn obliged to provide horses, and one has
frequently to wait until they can be brought from a distant farm.    At every station a dagbog or daybook is
kept, in which the traveler is at liberty to write any
complaint he may have to make.    This is periodically
inspected by the authorities, the charges are investigated, and the delinquents severely punished.    The carrioles seem well adapted to the character of the country
as they are so light that they safely pass over the
roughest roads; they may also be transported in boats
over the numerous fiords which intersect the many
routes.    Then it is a free and independent way of traveling.    One can go slow or fast or stop at discretion,
and thus can see everything the country affords to the
best advantage.

The stations I found to be much on the same plan.
They consist usually of but one or two small farm-
houses surrounded by a number of horse and cattle
stables and wood sheds.    A large room is always set

apart as a general parlor. This contains a little plain furniture; sometimes, though rarely a piano; always the photographs of the postmaster or station-keeper and his family; and the centre-table is often graced, in summer, with simple mountain flowers. The bed-rooms are small but clean; the beds invariably too narrow and too short, and carpets never adorn the floor. The kitchen is apt to contain a stove which has every appearance of having been made upon the premises and by a person who had not given his entire life to the theory and practice of this useful manufacture. Adjoining is a small pantry containing the few simple articles which are served to the famished traveler. One thus procures excellent trout and salmon, good eggs, cheese, and sometimes a pudding. Beef or mutton or pork is occasionally to be had, but is usually tough and always too much cooked. Preserved meats are sometimes proffered. The distinctively native and ever-recurring dishes are a species of sausage and flad-brod, a round, thin cake made of barley or rye, looking like coarse brown leather, and hence compared to the bottom of a hat-box with the paper stripped off. It is not excessively delicate or rich. You never fail to have ol, the light, spicy, and refreshing beer of Scandinavia.

But I fear the reader must be tired of this rambling introduction and I shall therefore begin at once the story of my long tour through Norway. I had decided upon that route across the southern part of the country already briefly described. Ninety miles by rail through

an undulating, agricultural region and a steamboat trip
up a beautiful little fiord, with surrounding hills reminding one of Lake Zurich, in Switzerland, brought me to
the beginning of my carriole journey.

# CHAPTER V.

## FIELD, FOSS, AND FIORD.

At first my road led through a thinly populated valley. The farm-houses were usually but one story in height, built of logs morticed together at the corners, with the seams stuffed with moss. The roof was made of birch bark covered with sod and huge stones. The windows were exceedingly small and few. The people I met invariably raised their hats, a custom much more agreeable than the stolid stare of other nations. The women were at work in the fields with the men, as is customary in most European countries. In gradually rising to the summit of the Fille Field, I left behind me the spruces and pines, and met instead willows, alders and birch. The hills became dark and naked. The wind and cold increased. Directly north of the posting-station here, and perhaps 30 miles distant, rises Mount Galdhopiggen, which is about 8,000 feet high, and the loftiest peak in Norway. The station-keeper offered to sell me some magnificent antlers of reindeer shot the previous autumn on the neighboring hills. A pair about four feet in length, with splendid terminal sprays, costs only $10. Some skins were also remarkably cheap, that of a bear $10, a deer $2.50, and a wolf $3. Near

the summit-level of the pass, I visited the rude house of
a herdsman. It was simply a little hovel of loose stones,
hardly high enough to stand upright in, and filled with
smoke which rose but feebly through an opening in the
roof, its only exit. This roof was composed of turf in
which were growing birch and alder trees. In a huge
kettle milk was boiling and in an adjoining closet
cheeses were placed in rows as in our presses at home.
These shepherds are very poor, their food consisting
almost entirely of oatmeal.

As I journeyed on, white-capped mountains appeared
on every hand, and huge snow-ploughs by the roadside
hinted of far different scenery in the winter time. The
snow then lies upon the ground in most places four feet
deep, and in some drifts one hundred feet. Roads are
then opened by snow-ploughs over the frozen fiords, as
being more level and more direct. Leaving the station
of Maristuen I entered a very wild cañon. Huge
masses of grayish rock towered 1,500 and 2,000 feet
above me. The roar of the torrent, swelled by numbers
of little streams and echoed from cliff to cliff, was almost
deafening. This pass is a yawning gulf which must
have cost nature terrific throes in its formation. The
various geological strata are interesting. Sometimes
you see blue quartz below and mica slate above, the
bottom rock being often upheaved to the very summit
of the slate. Some of the huge masses resemble the
lava torrents of Vesuvius. Others are formed of layers
bent into every conceivable shape, having numerous
"faults," and so frayed and scarred by the elements as

to present a most sombre and appalling picture. The gigantic boulders scattered about and the vast sand terraces passed lower down the stream would seem to indicate that the ocean had once penetrated far into this wondrous gorge.

Here also I saw many pretty peasant women, with their oval faces, soft gray eyes, and fair hair. Their holiday costume was very picturesque. It consisted of a dark bodice gayly trimmed with large buttons, a green skirt, immense apron, and silver brooches, earrings and shoe buckles. The men wore short jackets, fancy vests, knee breeches, and red worsted caps.

One of the oldest buildings in Norway is a church which was so near my route that I stopped to inspect it. It is said to date from the eleventh century and what is more singular it is built entirely of pine. Doubtless it is indebted largely for its preservation to the fact of its being annually coated with pitch. This stains it a dark red color. It is a most fantastic little building in the Byzantine and Romanesque styles of architecture. There are three tiers of receding roofs, of which the lower comes to within a few feet of the ground, covering a passage about three feet wide which runs entirely around the exterior. The gables of the roofs and the uppermost spire are ornamented with grotesque dragons and crosses. The entrance is encircled by some singular Runic carving, in which the dragon's head predominates, and the door-knocker and lock consist of iron-work recalling that of Nuremburg, in Germany. The nave is only about forty feet square and the chancel, which is perhaps half as large, is terminated by a semi-circular apse whose radius is but five feet. Here is the ancient stone altar. It is dimly lighted by several small windows. The situation of this quaint little church is most picturesque. It stands in the midst of a large meadow and at the extremity of a rather large opening in the valley, surrounded on every side by immense dark walls of rock.

After a pleasant experience of three days, I exchanged my carriole for a steamer—a little vessel hardly fifty feet in length—plying upon an upper arm of the Sogne fiord. This is the largest or at least the longest fiord in Norway, as it extends about 120 miles directly inland from the sea. The water is of an emerald hue and in some places over a mile in depth. With its numerous arms it may very appropriately be likened to the skeleton of a tree. It is in the smaller branches that the finest scenery is generally found. The friths of Western Scotland would convey but an imperfect idea of the Norway fiords. Those lack the diversity, the sublimity, and the gracefulness of these. The main trunk of Sogne fiord varies from half a mile to a mile in width, and the bordering hills range from 1,000 to 5,000 feet in height. Although its general direction is east and west, yet it is so tortuous in detail that one can never see far in advance. This, however, only serves to increase the interest, for scene follows upon scene with such rapidity that one never tires of gazing. The contrasts, too, as we steam along, are most remarkable. There is perpetual variety in form and feature. On the one side we have rough, almost barren hills capped with patches of snow ; on the other, a bright little dale with a few houses and cultivated fields. Or we see a range of densely wooded dark-green hills and just above them the glinting glaciers of some rocky summit. The stern, massive, immovable character of the stone hills forms a very striking comparison with the clear bosom of the sea, ruffled by just the faintest breeze. I constitute myself the figure-head of the little steamer as I take my seat directly upon the prow. The atmosphere is of crystal, not a cloud flecks the sky. The light certainly could not be more favorable for observing the master-pieces of nature placed so charmingly before me. What a region for an artist !

The steamer turns now into a little bay (ten miles in length and at its mouth, less than half a mile in width) called Naerofiord. Here the scenery becomes at once wildly romantic and savagely grand. At the right a vertical wall of hoary rock, without a patch of vegetation, rises perhaps 2,500 feet in the air. On the left the bluffs are covered with low scrub. We see no peaks, no pointed summits; the tops of the mountains all seem to be rounded and dome-shaped. The silver sheen of the water reflects to perfection the gray of the rock, the green of the birch trees, and the white of the snow-fields. In no part of the world have I ever seen mountains so clearly defined against the sky. Their lines are more diversified, their summits less smooth, their colors more varied, their vegetation less exuberant; in short, they are characterized by a greater number of peculiarities than are elsewhere to be found among mountains. The scene is at the same time appalling and enchanting. Cascades in some places fall from the tops of cliffs 1,500 feet in height, dashing themselves over the rough rocks in liquid splinters and opalescent foam, through which the sun strikes myriad rainbows. The sides of the hills are everywhere worn into gullies by descending torrents. One also observes chains of slender falls and round hollowed basins. Some of the mountains are said to actually attain the height of a mile. The extreme transparency of the atmosphere, however, renders the seeming height less than the real, and so the story wears a trifle of the incredible. The sea reflects everything most marvelously. One sees the entire panorama by simply gazing into the water. The forms of the mountains and their colors seem reflected still more sharply within the water than they absolutely are in themselves. When a snow-capped mountain, in its entirety, is for the first time beheld reversed in the sea, the effect is bewildering. Spell-bound I sat, and if my eyes had been fifty instead of two, I should have found an excellent use for all.

We pass occasionally clusters of huts and see sometimes a farm two thousand feet above the fiord; but one has little interest for weak man or his puny affairs in presence of the sublime and wonderful works of nature. Such sheer precipices, such woody slopes, such effects of light and shade! It is as though they were beheld in some gigantic vision. It is wonderland. The nerves thrill with the enchantment of the brain.

But how terrible would such a place become without the glittering transfiguration of the sun! At night, seen only by the light of stars and moon, the scene must be fantastically weird, like one of nature's nightmares.

At the head of Naerofiord I land and continue my journey in a sort of vehicle which is sometimes used in place of a carriole on good mountain roads. It is a very primitive affair with four low wheels and scarcely any perceptible springs. The body is simply a huge box, with two seats having backs a couple of feet in height and covered with hide. The horses are attached by wooden shafts instead of a central pole and traces as with us. The way wound along a raging torrent and up a deep valley, the sides of which rose high above our heads. One mountain was an immense cone of steep, polished gray stone, which towered proudly above the valley, and seemed calculated to last an eternity. The formation of this peak is peculiar, the strata of one-half of it being horizontal and those of the other vertical. Going on, we seem to be shut in by the abrupt termination of the valley, but nature has left there a rather steep hill, up which, by a most masterly piece of engineering, a road has been constructed by a Norwegian officer. This difficult and costly undertaking was accomplished by means of eighteen bends of solid masonry, thus zigzagging about a thousand feet upward to a plateau which connects with another valley. The road doubles or rather quadruples upon itself, with scarcely its own width between, in a distance of a hundred feet. On both sides of it are fine waterfalls, each about four hundred feet in height, so that in making the ascent of this precipitous portion of the road, when you compare the falls with one another, the element of height must be omitted.

As we advance the valley widens, the vegetation becomes more dense, larger cultivated fields and more habitations appear, though the latter all seem dilapidated. Oats and potatoes meet the eye and much hay is being harvested. After being cut, the grass is spread upon birch twig racks, which being raised a few feet from the ground, prevent wet or dampness and also allow a free circulation of the air, so that with the assistance of the sun, a much better opportunity for drying is afforded than by our process of curing in the United States. In some farms where the ground is very steep, a long wire is stretched from the distant hill-tops by which bundles of hay are sent down to or near the barn, thus saving much arduous transportation. A drive of about fifty miles brought me to the Hardanger fiord, the second in Norway in point of size and scenery, though its cataracts and glaciers and fertile valleys, and frequent transitions from the grand and sublime to the soft and lovely, almost entitle it to the first consideration.

The most remarkable of the branches of this great fiord is that extending some twenty-five miles southward to the little village of Odde. Like Naerofiord it is bounded on either side by almost unbroken mountain walls from 3,000 to 4,000 feet in height, though they are

less steep and more wooded than the former. There
are many farms and rich orchards lying in narrow strips
along the lower parts of these mountains. Here and
there one gets a peep up a fairy vale, with cataracts
leaping from rock to rock as if the hills were embroidered with silver threads. The fiord at first is perhaps
a mile in width; the water is of a dark green hue and
remarkably cold, being fed by many glacier streams.
We have a magnificent view of the Folgefond mountain with its shining expanse of snow, upon the right;
and upon the left, a smiling valley with clusters of
farms, and a small waterfall which makes a great perpendicular leap at an altitude of about 2,000 feet. This
is a frequent and always striking feature of the Norwegian landscape. We see the glorious glaciers of the
Folgefond with their light blue ice a hundred feet in
depth, and their snow-fields extending for miles—an
enormous winding-sheet of white.

Odde is a pretty village of about a dozen houses, in
one of which I was most hospitably entertained for a
few days. From there I made a delightful little excursion up the Gromsdal valley, about twenty miles southeast, by an excellent road. I first drove around a large
lake, across which were continually to be had splendid
views of the famous Buerbrae glacier, with its immense
wall of pale blue ice descending low into a bright fertile valley. This glacier, which has been forming during the past half century, is still increasing in extent,
and threatens to destroy the farm at its foot. In 1870
it advanced 250 feet, and during a single week in the

following year, as much as twelve feet. Its lower edge
is now only about 800 feet above the lake. Leaving
the latter, I sped merrily along the side of a big bub-
bling brook which at first wound through a vale of lux-
uriantly lovely vegetation and then the scene suddenly
changed to a gorge of high rocky mountains, with a little stunted shrubbery and many thundering cataracts.
This gorge is said to be one of the grandest in Norway
and I am quite ready to indorse the claim. Yet it
would be difficult to give specific and exact reasons for
its attractiveness. Nothing abounds but purple rocks
and dwarfish birches, alternating with the shivering
sheen of mighty cascades. The forms of the hills are
most diversified. Throughout its length the cañon is
nearly choked by vast avalanches of stone which the
frost has started from the cliffs—huge boulders, some
of them thirty and even forty feet square, piled together in a complete chaos of confusion, or else rolled
down the mountain slopes, very Niagaras of stone. A
passage for the road has even had to be blasted through
some of these rock floes. A waterfall hard by is nearly
a thousand feet in height Its companions are the two
beautiful cataracts of Laathefoss, which blind with
their spray and deafen with their roar. Two other fine
cataracts, one of them 500 feet high and 100 feet wide,
may be seen from the same spot. A few miles farther
up this unique gorge the government has selected a
spot which is deemed to be in the best position for obtaining a view of the great Folgefond. Upon this site
is erected a platform which supports a metal Norwegian

flag, and whence can be seen the Folgefond, appearing to unfold into four mountain ridges. First come the green sub-hills ; next, a range with a very little snow upon it ; then appears a crest which is much higher and whiter ; and finally one beholds the snow-capped outline of the loftiest peaks or rather domes, for that, as I have said, is the form assumed by nearly all the mountains of Norway. A most beautiful sight was the enormous field of ermine which lay extended before my entranced eyes ; but no, I will not call it ermine, for this specimen of nature's dazzling integrity was never stained. The picture is equal to any in the Tyrol.

Another day, a rainy one, not being suitable for mountain views, but quite as good, if not better, for observing waterfalls, was employed in a trip, with a guide, to what may perhaps be styled the lion of Norwegian cataracts, the Ringdalfoss or the Rounded Waterfall, so named from its general appearance. We first row four miles down the fiord, with splendid spectacles of snow, rock and forest continually around. Then we land and climb up a narrow valley along the precipitous banks of a brawling brook skirted by fir trees. Behind, we look upon the summits of the Folgefond. In a couple of hours we reach a dilapidated farm-house, the owner whereof rents us his skiff in order to cross a large lake, at the further extremity of which is the great Ringdalfoss waterfall. Before this is reached, however, there is a beautiful double-fall which alone would well repay the troubles of the rough ascent of the valley. The lake is surrounded by lofty and steep slate walls, with quartz strata, and a mingling also of purple granite. The fall consists of two streams which descending from different parts of the precipice join each other about two-thirds of the distance down, thus making a perfectly-shaped Y. They start very sharply defined from the top but at the bottom melt into the very lightest clouds of water-dust. In clear weather of course this spray forms rainbows of great beauty. The wedded cascades plunge into a small but very deep basin and before reaching the lake take together another jump of perhaps two hundred feet.

The Ringdalfoss comes with a tremendous rush over the precipice in an immense body of water, and falls, 850 feet of spray and foam, into "a gulf profound" of dark rocks, and thence flows, with another but comparatively low leap and a width of 200 feet, directly into the lake. This truly magnificent fall is fed by a number of small lakes high up in the mountains and they in turn by streams flowing from the ever-present snow. You can land and scramble over heaps of debris to the very foot of the Ringdalfoss where, although the spray is almost blinding, as you look directly upward to the ridge of rock, the water appears to rush far out and to hang for an instant in mid-air as if uncertain whether it were best to take such a fearful bound. But the great law of gravitation is not to be violated and down it comes, a monstrous avalanche of sparkling snow, and strikes the abyss with a cry of thunder. All is misty and wet and dismal around, and the black sombre cliff towers above ; but down below, not far beneath your feet, are the placid lake, a few plots of cultivated land, and some brightly-blooming wild flowers. We push our boat off from the slate-shingle shore and row slowly back, the grand old fall, touched with a Protean spirit, putting on a different aspect at the separation produced by almost every dozen additional strokes of our oars.

Norway is the fatherland of waterfalls. In summer many of them have too little water to produce a beautiful effect, and in spring and winter, when the rivers and lakes are full, it is often dangerous to reach the falls because of the terrible avalanches which then prevail. I saw many interesting proofs of the power of frost in tearing down mountains and hurling the fragments far into the valleys. Some of the huge boulders must have been thrown down centuries ago judging from the full-sized trees now growing upon them ; while others, at present perhaps lying in the midst of fertile fields, but a few months ago formed the surface wall of the neighboring mountain. In fact, our globe is gradually and, owing to its great size, of course, almost imperceptibly altering its configuration and becoming smoother and more rotund. Two grand agents are constantly at work in effecting this change. These are (1) denudation, which is always abrading and carrying to a lower level the exposed surfaces, and (2) an internal force, like that of volcanoes, which is raising or depressing the existing strata or bringing unstratified rock to the exterior.

In order to reach the steamer bound for the sea-board city of Bergen, it was necessary for me to be rowed

down the fiord about twenty-five miles, to its nearest
calling-place. Upon arrival the steamer proved to be
quite small, and was crowded with passengers. We
stopped at many hamlets. There seemed to be very
little fertile land and but few settlers. Now we passed
through a crooked channel scarcely wider than the
steamer; again we were in an almost land-locked bay,
with dark bluffs frowning upon us. We passed many
fishing-smacks at anchor near the land and, off-shore,
several fleets of small boats which were engaged in
"drifting" for herring. These boats frequent the entire coast and prove excellent sea-craft. The building
of them is one of the chief sources of income to the
inhabitants of Hardanger fiord.

We had been for some time steering directly to the
north when, on suddenly rounding a headland, we saw
before us a long line of white warehouses with mighty
masses of rock rising behind them; a great fleet of
quaint looking boats and a dozen or more little steamers
in front; a fort upon each of two long narrow penin-
sulas, one on the right and the other on the left; and
beyond, in a semi-circle, the houses and churches of
the second city of Norway—Bergen. I at once landed
and without difficulty succeeded in finding a very good
hotel.

# CHAPTER VI.

## Two Old Norse Cities.

BERGEN is situated in about the same degree of latitude as Christiania. Founded some eight hundred
years ago, it was for a long time the capital of Norway
and a place of great commercial importance, but now
its trade is decreasing at about the same rate as that at
which the trade of Christiania is increasing. To-day it
has a population of 40,000. Very many of the houses,
mostly built of timber, and with sharply-peaked roofs,
are placed with their gable-ends toward the streets.
The latter are very irregular though well-paved. Some
are quite steep and all such have a special track with
stones tilted up so as to afford a footing for the horses.
In wandering through the chief thoroughfares, which
are filled with a great variety of shops, one is often
startled by the appearance of policemen garbed almost
the same as those met with in London. Formerly they
had here a species of night watchmen armed with a
most villainous and death-dealing weapon which (like
too many of the New York policemen) they were not
slow to employ upon slight pretexts. This weapon was
a staff similar to the heavy mace used in the days of
chivalry. It was about four feet in length, having at

the end a huge ball of brass set with spikes half an inch in length. This beautiful little toy was termed by the would-be-facetious a "morning star."

Bergen has much of a German aspect. This is owing to the fact that for many years the Germans held here the monopoly of the northern fishing trade. In walking through the market I saw nothing for sale save fish, potatoes, and firewood. The people, when ordering their dinners, never need to imitate the example of the Catholics in considering what day of the week it may be, for it seems to be always Friday and fast-day fare with them. The chief trade of Bergen is in dried cod-fish (called stock-fish), cod-liver oil and herrings. The huge warehouses, where the dried fish are corded up like wood, face upon a broad street parallel with the harbor, and extend a long distance backward, having only very narrow passage-ways between. It is unfortunate that these should all be built of wood, for if they and their tinder-like contents should once get on fire, it would be next to impossible to save them. In fact, the same might justly be said of all Bergen, which has been several times nearly consumed by fire. Though the warehouses exhale "a very ancient and fish-like smell," this alone was not a sufficiently great obstacle to deter an inquiring mind from the pursuit of knowledge.

The codfish are sent to the Mediterranean ports; the herrings are mostly consumed in the Baltic; while the cod-liver oil goes to all parts of Europe and America. Much of the fish trade of Norway is in the hands of the merchants of Bergen, who export nearly every year

more than $2,000,000 worth of codfish, 600,000 barrels
of pickled herrings, and 20,000 barrels of cod-liver oil.
Along the wharves one sees many of the great boats
which are engaged in bringing the fish from the Loffoden islands and Finmark, the best fishing grounds.
These boats called Jachts (whence our modern Yacht),
are very curiously constructed. They range from fifty
to two hundred tons in burden, are very broad, and
have a mast in the centre which supports a huge square
sail and a small top-sail. Their bows are curved very
high, so that the helmsman may see them when the
intermediate space is filled with a large cargo. When
sailing before the wind these jachts need only a bank
or two of oars to make them exactly resemble the gal-
leys of the old piratical Northmen.

The chief attraction of Bergen is found in its picturesque and quaint appearance and situation. It is so
uneven and so surrounded by mountains that you frequently find the outlines of a street statue stand out
upon them as against a background. This peculiar
effect is also to be seen at Innspruck, in the Tyrol.
There is in Bergen a museum, containing a small
though excellent collection of mementoes of the Northmen ; a cabinet of natural history ; and a picture-gal-
lery. In the streets one occasionally sees some of the
old fantastic costumes of the peasantry, though these
are now generally reserved for Sundays, holidays or
weddings. In the jewellers' shops I noticed several
gilt and silver crowns, which in my innocent ignorance
I imagined had been placed on sale, or perhaps pawned,

by some Viking now retired from business. I afterwards learned that these were worn by brides for several days after the wedding, and that the nuptial festivi-
ties were finally terminated by dancing until these orna-
mental badges of dignity fell off,—a rather difficult ac-
complishment, were it not that they are so cleverly constructed that upon the withdrawal of a certain pin they
at once fall of themselves to the ground.   Posted about
the city were bills giving notice that Mr. Ole Bull would
give a series of concerts.   This celebrated and lamented
violinist was born here and resided at the time of his
death in the suburbs.   Bergen itself cannot be a very
healthy place in which to live as the proximity of the
mountains renders it very subject to rain.   In fact, they
have here over two hundred days of rain during the
year, and the official statistics place the annual fall at
seventy inches.   Bergen, however, impressed me as what
a Yankee would term a "regular live town."   The
stores were stocked with the greatest variety of goods,
and the people jostled one another in the streets in the
eager rush and turmoil of business activity.

A fortnightly line of steamers is established between
Bergen and New York, and frequent communication is
maintained with all the coast towns of Norway.   Two
lines of steamers run to North Cape, and another
goes still farther, to Vadso, near the Russian boundary,
a distance of about 2,000 miles from Christiania.   In
selecting one of these lines and taking my passage for
the North Cape, I must confess to having felt something
of a flutter of the heart ; for I was thus committed to

the extreme north of Europe, past the Arctic Circle, out of reach of most of the comforts of civilized life, also beyond its fevered bustle, away up to the homes of the Lapps and the Reindeer, even to the veritable land of the Aurora Borealis and the Midnight Sun.

I found but few passengers in a fine iron steamer of some 500 tons burden, which was built at Bergen. Our route was nearly due north between the main land and the islands which form, as it were, a gigantic break-water along the entire western coast of Norway. The navigation is at all times intricate and dangerous but becomes especially so in foggy weather. Two pilots are taken the entire distance from Bergen to Hammer-fest. The steamers are guided through the mazes of the coast islands by a pilot on the bridge, who simply motions with his hands to the helmsman "starboard" or "port." Most of the distance to North Cape is per-formed in the fiords but a part, especially in the more northerly section, is exposed to the full sweep of the North Atlantic. The outer fringe of islands is well-lighted throughout the entire length of the Norwegian coast, and the marine charts are admirably drawn after the most accurate surveys. The islands and islets sometimes appear to be only projections of the main-land, though a nearer approach dispels the illusion ; or again, they lie so closely together that no outlet seems possible, till another turn shows an opening between them, with a glimpse of the sea beyond. The steamers run throughout the year, being provided with steam-pipes and stoves against the severe cold of the winter.

The cargo taken up the coast consists of groceries and various manufactured articles, and that taken down is composed of fish and oil.

The first town of any great importance at which we stop is Christiansand, situated upon three small islands which together form a completely land-locked harbor. The population is but 7,000. We drop anchor among a few ships and many small fishing smacks. The shore is lined with huge fish-warehouses, some of which are five stories in height. I ask the captain if there is any-thing special to be seen on shore, and he replies " yes, a park with three trees, a few rocks, and some dried fish."

Christiansand seems to have a character of its own apart from other Norwegian towns. It is so irregularly built that no two houses appear to be upon the same level. Some are reached by ascending, others by de-scending, long flights of stairs. In short, so diversified is the surface of this town that a complete view of it is impossible. I pass a fine large wooden church whose two clock-dials are at least double-faced enough to give me a widely diverging choice of time. The captain, I found, had been guilty of a libel on the park, for it con-tained many trees which, though small, made an agree-able shade, and there were also many beds of beautiful flowers. It was a fruitful little oasis in a genuine desert of rock. Children, as is usual in Norwegian towns, swarmed everywhere, and the men would stop in the streets and look at me with as much curiosity as if I had been a North American Indian in full war paint and feathers, or as though Europeans had not been travelling in Norway for a century past. After receiving on board a little cargo, we steam out of the harbor and soon are headed again towards the north. It was the height of the summer herring fishery and we passed a great fleet of smacks, some going up empty to the grounds, others coming down with their cargoes. The boats make a very quaint appearance at sea, recalling to my mind that of the Japanese junks. Some of them have only the large square sails like the jachts at Bergen. These sail well before the wind but are so shallow as to fall much away when beating to windward. Others, most picturesque of all, are arrayed with mainsail, top-sail, and three jibs. Just before we reached Trondjhem, at midnight, the light was sufficiently clear and strong to enable me to write a letter upon the deck of the steamer.

Like Bergen, Trondjhem was for a long time the capital of Norway, but now it is the third city, its population being about 21,000. Four times has the whole of it been laid in ashes, being built of wood, though in future all new buildings must be made of brick or stone. The great glory of Trondjhem is its old cathedral where the kings have always been crowned. I turn from my hotel, a very comfortable one arranged somewhat in the English style, into the main street, which runs from the harbor directly to the cathedral, passing the palace where the kings reside during the coronation ceremonies, a plain two-story barrack of wood. Then I reach the market-place, which is simply the intersec-

tion of two streets filled with portable booths and carts
of fish and vegetables. As in Bergen, you look from
the centre of the streets up to the hills on three sides,
and on the fourth, out upon the green waters of the
fiord. Part of the cathedral, which stands at one extremity of the city, in the midst of a large cemetery, is
in ruins, caused by the devastating fires which have so
often visited the place. The work of restoration is now
in progress. What we see of the old portions, which
are in the simple style of Norman architecture with
semi-circular arches, massive columns and varied sculptures, gives an idea of the magnificence of the cathedral when entire. It was then 350 feet in length and 85
in breadth, but two chapels increased the width of one
front to 140 feet. It is cruciform and is built of a dark
slate-colored stone found in the vicinity. Parts of it
are seven hundred years old and contain most curious
statues and busts.

This cathedral was first built as a shrine over a certain Olaf, the patron saint of Norway. Olaf was an old
Norse king, who, dying at the moment of victory over
some rude tribes of the north, was afterwards raised
to the dignity of martyr and worshipped accordingly.
Pilgrimages were soon made to his grave from all parts
of Scandinavia, and so great was the veneration in
which he was held, and so widely was he known, that
churches were erected to his memory even in Constantinople. The present king of Sweden and Norway,
Oscar II., was crowned, together with his queen, in this
cathedral, in 1872. The restoration which progresses

very slowly, owing to the lack of subscriptions, is of a much lighter and more graceful type of architecture, closely resembling the Gothic, with its sharply pointed arches and clustered columns. It does not seem to harmonize well with the great size, elevation, simplicity and strength of the old Norman style.

Nearly all the graves about the cathedral were covered with vases of flowers, most of which were quite fresh, and each of the plots contained benches which seemed to have been diverted from their original purpose to that of public lounging-places, before and after the neighboring religious service. I was surprised and shocked, but afterwards learned that Norway and Sweden, following the example of Turkey, use their necropoli as pleasure parks in which the people sit and sleep, talk and joke, eat and drink. And in truth these burial-grounds seem better adapted to the amusement of the living than the repose of the dead, for they are crossed by paths, ornamented with groves and flower-beds, and provided with sufficient seats to accommodate their vivacious visitors.

In returning to my hotel I met a funeral procession. I had noticed that the street was covered with fir boughs, but supposed it was in honor of some church fête. First came an open hearse drawn by two horses led by grooms, all draped in the deepest black. The coffin, however, was completely covered with flowers of all colors, so much so in fact that it could not be seen. Behind, four abreast, all in black clothes, with silk hats, walked the male relatives and friends. In Norway, as in Denmark, women never appear as mourners in funeral processions, not even at the burial of members of their own sex.

There is a church in Trondjhem similar to one in Copenhagen, which is worthy of a visit. The congregation have evidently increased — so much so, that rather than erect a new edifice, they have built upon each side two rows of pews, like opera-boxes, reaching nearly to the ceiling. Each of these boxes is entered directly from the outside, as is the pulpit, which extends a long distance from the wall into the body of the church. Above and behind the pulpit is a huge carved altar-piece which is colored in very tawdry style This church bears date 1729. Besides the expected churches there is a good museum, library, and reading-room in the city. The country about Trondjhem is very fertile, producing large harvests of oats, corn, potatoes and hay.

To travel by the railway to Christiania uses up the daylight of two days, the trains not running at night. This singular custom is admirable for those who wish to see the country, but must prove rather disagreeable to merchants who desire to use dispatch both in traveling and in forwarding goods. From Trondjhem there is a very fine road, with good posting stations, across Norway and Sweden to Sundsvall, a town on the Gulf of Bothnia This road is about 350 miles in length From Sundsvall to Stockholm, the distance by steamer cannot be more than 300 miles. At Trondjhem Norway has narrowed to something like eighty miles in width, and from here to Tromsoe it is a mere strip of land, or rock rather, bordering the ocean. About latitude sixty-nine degrees north, the boundary line dips a little further into the interior, embracing the district styled Finmark, but soon again it returns northward and so continues on to the shores of the Polar Sea.

# CHAPTER VII.

## OFF AND ON THE COAST.

ONE'S sensations in traversing distant and little-fre-
quented lands are often curious, sometimes amusing.
I have already referred to the state of mind in which I
left Bergen, with the psychical effect of the steamer's
prow headed toward the mysterious Pole. In depart-
ing from Trondjhem, although that city was so much
nearer my goal, yet it rather seemed as though I were
leaving the frontiers of the civilized world, and simply
going to a few advanced stations whither pioneers had
but recently ventured, to see if there might be aught in
the land to tempt a following.

However, we were soon at the mouth of the Nam-
sen, one of the best salmon rivers in the country, and
entirely leased to English sportsmen, as indeed are
nearly all the other good shooting and fishing localities.
Norway is, or at least was a few years ago, a genuine
sportsman's paradise. When I heard of the size and
"gameness" of the fish, and of the varieties and number of the birds and quadrupeds it produces, I much
regretted that my *batterie de la chasse* was far away at
home, and that I had simply come to "spy out the
land."

The next day we passed a famous mountain called Torghattan, which is of bare rock and resembles in shape a sailor's "sou'-wester hat." It is a grand dome-shaped mass about eight hundred feet in height and is noted for a natural orifice or tunnel which passes quite through it from side to side. The rock is gneiss and the opening, which has been produced by the disintegration of a vein of mica, is 520 feet long, 60 feet wide, and 100 feet high. Its walls are quite smooth, but its roof is jagged, while its bottom consists of sharp-pointed pieces of granite. Upon the mainland the mountains also lie in jagged and irregular groups. They are bare rocks, many of them with patches of snow upon their summits. The scene is utterly desolate, and yet in every green patch of fifty square feet I was sure to see a fisherman's hut. The rocks of these very mountains, however, purpled by the setting sun, and with their snow fields of a like delicate tinge, with a foreground of dark water, form a really magnificent sight.

In Norway I frequently contrasted the appearance of mountains when viewed from lakes or the sea with that presented from valleys, and found that the advantage of having a sharply-defined water-line in a mountain view is very great. If it be allowable to compare the works of Nature with those of Art, I should liken the elements of majesty and repose, expressed in the Norwegian Alps, to the same qualities produced by means of long level lines contrasted with perpendicular or nearly perpendicular lines, in the ancient architecture of Egypt.

We were now coasting along that province of Norway called Nordland. This extends in a longitudinal
direction for about fifty miles and is from forty to sixty
miles in width. Its population is estimated at 100,000.
Though its interior has not yet been thoroughly ex-
plored, it is undoubtedly one of the most interesting
parts of the country. It contains huge mountains, immense glaciers, vast stalactite caverns, subterranean
rivers, marble hills, iron and silver ores, great falls, and
much wild and rugged as well as soft and graceful
scenery. At a little village where we stopped were
many barrows—ancient stone monuments arranged in
concentric circles somewhat similar to those at Stonehenge in Wiltshire, England. The origin of these has
been the subject of much discussion. After still closer
study they are doubtless destined to throw light upon
the early history of the country. To the northeast we
see the snow mountains of Svartisen, with their giant
glaciers glittering in the brilliant rays of the sun.

There would seem to be three grand glacier systems
in Norway. The most extensive is that of the Justedal
range, lying north of the Sogne fiord. This covers an
area of about eighty square miles. The lower edge of
its snow-and-ice fields averages about 4,000 feet above
sea-level, though two of them descend, the one to 400,
the other to 150, feet above the same plane. The
greatest altitude of this range is 6,500 feet. The Svartisen, which ranks second in point of size, extending
along the coast for a distance of forty miles, is believed
to cover a surface of seventy square miles. The greater

part of it lies within the Arctic Circle. The third and last glacier system is that lying near the Hardanger fiord —the Folgefond—which is over 5,000 feet in height, but only covers about fifteen square miles.

Steaming up a beautiful fiord, we anchor near the townlet of Mo. I go on shore in a long narrow boat, which is turned up at each end like the birch canoes of the American Indians. It is Sunday and I am going to church. Scene on the right : many large boats arriving at the landing filled with people all clad in their best clothes, as is customary on the Sabbath in other Christian countries. Scene on the left : a small whale amusing himself by swallowing some shoals of herrings, with flocks of sea-birds hovering in the air above ready to dart upon any that might perchance escape the capacious maw of the marine monster, lashing the water as if there he were undisputed monarch. I walk through a village of perhaps fifty dwellings, most of them mere wooden huts with turf roofs, a few being frame houses painted red. The winding road is filled with people going in the same direction as myself—namely, to the kirke. This I find to be a large red edifice with long windows and an odd cupola, built of logs morticed at the corners and the seams wadded with moss. There is no sexton in attendance, and so I walk in and seat myself on the women's side, for the men occupy one side and the women the other in a Norwegian church. My apparently mistaken situation seemed, however, to much disturb a few coy little maidens sitting near. With their restless blue eyes and fair hair combed straight back from the forehead and half concealed beneath gay-colored bandannas, they certainly were very bewitching. But while in the presence of heavenly glories it was clearly morally obligatory on me to withstand the fascination of those that, however beautifully feminine, were still earthly. So I endeavored to preserve a stately and severe demeanor, no easy task under the conditions. Even the sermon in which I at last despairingly sought refuge from the varied seductions of the charming creatures, failed me, for, owing to the rapidity of the worthy pastor's delivery and my own scanty stock of Norsk, I could hardly understand a single sentence. I have mentally vowed never again to endeavor to rival the hero of "The Pirates of Penzance" in my doughty devotion to duty.

Within, the cruciform church was of plain deal with a narrow gallery running entirely around it. Before the altar, with its large gaudy paintings, stood the pastor in a black gown and black stockings. Around his neck he wore a white ruffed collar standing out somewhat after the style of those which we see in the pictures of good Queen Bess. He was engaged apparently in the confirmation of several members of his flock, for he repeated some ordinances, placing his hands upon the head of each person at the altar, and afterwards shook hands with all.

The clergy of Norway are learned men, as they have to pass severe examinations before being ordained. The average salary they receive is about $1,000 per annum. Many of the women were pretty, though all those of middle age gave unmistakable signs of lives of hardship and exposure. The men had the appearance of hardy toilers of the sea. They were clad in oil-skin breeches and pea-jackets, with tarpaulin hats. What surprised me was the continual going in and out of both men and women during the service. There were many chants and responses, and the pastor exchanged his black for a white gown, somewhat after the manner of the Episcopal ministers. They sang many hymns, a man standing near the altar, leading. These were rendered apparently from memory, both words and melody, for very few had any books. The singing was not altogether unmusical, though many of the women's voices were quite harsh and sharp. After the singing, which was continued for nearly half an hour, the pastor harangued them for an equally long period, and then the morning service was concluded. It had doubtless been devout, but a certain new-comer had found it also dull and dismal.

Boat-building seemed to be the chief employment of the population of Mo. Their boats, built of pine, are from ten to thirty feet in length, and being sharp at each end, are admirably adapted to brave the surf. The villagers apparently do not want for a modicum of amusement to ease their toil. In returning to the steamer I was somewhat startled at seeing an oil painting attached to the exterior of a large house. It was a representation of two negresses. The one was a middle-aged woman adorned with gold earrings, locket, watch and chain, and dressed in a brown silk that

would make Worth die of mortification and envy. The
other figure was that of a little girl draped in white
satin, with a necklace of immense pearls, and carrying
a parasol. I of course appreciated the taste in the
selection of jewels : yellow gold for the brown silk, and
pearls for the white satin. In the background were a
piano with music, and a parrot upon his perch. I
looked at the grinning bystanders for a pantomimic
interpretation thereof, and they pointed to a bill posted
upon the house, which began in good Norsk (but only
fair English) " Kom og se ! " This was evidently
" Come and see." It was repeated twice, and then
followed some explanatory matter which I could not
decipher, though towards the end a single line threw
a coruscating light around the whole. This was " Fra
Mobilabama ved Mississippi-Floden.   12 skill." I
now understood that there was a highly moral ethnographical show in town, nothing less than two negresses
from Mobile, Alabama, near (*sic*) the Mississippi River.
The admittance fee was inexorably placed at four
cents.

The moral reflections in which I indulged suggested
to me that there was scarcely a place on earth without
some approximation, however distant, to a "show."
Here were these dark vagrants, mother and child, perhaps, whose ancestry flourished in the heart of Africa,
making a living out of their complexion and advertis-
ing their natural pigment on the verge of the Arctic
Circle and almost within the shadow of the Pole.

# CHAPTER VIII.

### Crossing the Arctic Circle.

We returned down the fiord and once again directed our prow toward the north. We passed many interesting mountains, some of them piled mass upon mass, others sloping as if they were of molten lead and about to rush away. The strata of some were tilted in every conceivable direction, as if they had been thrown up from a volcano, and like lava, suddenly become cool and stiff. We could easily accept the statement that they were formed at the creation of the world,—for no experience in world-making could have begotten such evolutionless monsters. As usual, wherever there was a patch of vegetation there also a hut appeared, and wherever three or four huts were visible, small fleets of fishing-smacks were to be seen lying at anchor. We now began to observe many flocks of sea-birds, consisting chiefly of gulls and ducks. But when the eye was not thus distracted, it everywhere lit upon grim savage mountains covered with snow, and low bare rocks rising from the sea. It was grand scenery, but without the frequent contrast of bright wooded valleys and soft fertile plains, became at length absolutely dispiriting.

We glide swiftly on past the ever-changing coast.

We leave behind the island of Lovunen with its great
dark sugar-loaf summit towering up from the water.
We pass the Threnen Islands, four sharp little peaks
rising abruptly from the sea, like The Needles of the
English Channel. We see the famous mountain called
Hestmando, which is about 1,500 feet in height. This
is the peak which is supposed by some people to represent a horseman swimming in the water. Such people,
however, must have been possessed of a species of
Arabian Nights' imagination, for I could not detect
the slightest resemblance to either horse or rider. It
is said that the Norwegian fishermen, who are quite
superstitious, take off their hats when their boats pass
this island.

The mountains increase in ruggedness as we cross
the Arctic Circle, in the meridian of thirteen degrees east
from Greenwich. We were then in a little higher latitude than the extreme northern point of Iceland. The
impression made upon the mind by entering the frigid
zone is peculiar, yet not indescribable. It is naturally
very different from that received in passing the equator.
There you are still in a sublunary paradise, but here
you are passing into a region of desolation and gloom.
There you are on or near some of the highways of the
world, but here you seem to be leaving behind everything that makes life worth having. There it is fair
and warm, here cold and stormy. To cross the polar
circle is really to enter another world—a grand and in a
way, a picturesque world, but one teeming with risks of
suffering, danger and death. It is doubtless superfluous

to tell my readers that this is the most southerly point from which the midnight sun may be seen at the level of the sea. Within this parallel the disk of the sun remains wholly above the horizon for a term of more than twenty-four hours at one season of the year, or does not rise for a term of more than twenty-four hours at the opposite period of the year.

Our steamer stops an hour at Bodo, a town of a thousand inhabitants and the capital of Nordland. Its situation near the fishing banks of Loffoden makes it a place of considerable commercial importance. It is the usual Norwegian fishing town, a few frame and many log houses, some wide streets, half a dozen meagre stores, and a score of fish and oil warehouses. Near this town stands the old parsonage in which Louis Philippe resided for some time during his exile. His room, decorated in the antique. style, is still shown. The scenery all about Bodo is of the wildest and most picturesque character. From here we steer north and west across the mouth of Vest Fiord, the largest fiord in Norway, to the Loffodens, about eighty miles distant. These islands are simply steep mountains, with peaks from two to three thousand feet in height, tipped with snow. Their serrated edges somewhat resemble the jaws of a shark.

The world-famous fishing banks, where for more than two hundred years the Norwegians have captured fish for domestic and foreign use, lie along the eastern shores of the Loffodens for a distance of a hundred miles. There are three ledges of different depths which

extend far out into the fiord, and here the codfish come
to spawn, because here they are protected from the
winds and waves.  They are caught during the months
of February and March, from open boats.  Generally
long gill-nets are joined together and sunk to the bottom of the sea, and the fish becoming entangled in
them are caught in great numbers.  The largest fish
are always taken in this manner.  Trawls, however, are
also extensively employed.  These are long lines, sometimes extending a mile or more along the ocean, and
having short lines with baited hooks attached to them.
As a rule the Loffoden fishery cannot be carried on
more than two days in a week, owing to the stormy
weather which is prevalent during its periodical progress.  The nets are usually left out several days at a
time, the fishermen visiting them each morning and
removing the fish that have been enmeshed the night
previous.  Sometimes as many as a thousand fish are
caught in a single night.  None are caught except at
night.

The gill-net system of Norway was recently introduced to the knowledge of our New England coast
fishermen, to whom the question of bait has become a
more and more serious one for years past.  But hardly
had it been fairly brought to their notice than, with
characteristic Yankee ingenuity, a plan was hit upon
whereby one man is enabled to accomplish the amount
of work for which seven men are required in Norway !
That was inevitable.  If a Cape Cod man had been
present at the creation he would probably have sug-

gested some important improvements in the working of the universe.

In Norway some of the fish are dried by the sun upon the flat rocks of the coast, but the greater part by both sun and air, being hung upon wooden frames specially constructed for this purpose. About midsummer the fish are properly cured and are then sent south as the stock-fish of commerce. The codfish, both dried and salted, are exported, as I have already stated, to France, Spain, and Italy. Cod roes go to France and Spain, where they are used in the capture of sardines. The herring fishery, which is also a source of great revenue to Norway, though it varies greatly, is carried on upon the southwest coast in the summer and autumn. The arrival of the shoals off the coast is instantly telegraphed from town to town. In good years as many as 600,000 barrels of herrings are shipped to Sweden, Denmark and the Baltic ports. There is a small white whale fishery north of the Loffodens. There is also a shark fishery for oil. This is carried on, however, further north, near Hammerfest. A shark's liver will yield from fifteen to sixty gallons of oil. At Spitzbergen and Nova Zembla, in the Polar ocean, are quite extensive seal fisheries. There are 25,000 men in Norway engaged in the cod fishery. The people living on the west coast are almost entirely supported by it. As many as 25,000,000 cod have been caught in sixty days! This fishery is quite regular, but the herring fishery never can be depended on. In 1874 only 17,000 barrels of herring were taken, the average annual yield having previously been about 600,000 barrels.  For some undiscovered reason the herring fishery is rapidly decreasing.

One by one the fondly cherished beliefs of childhood are cruelly dispelled.  Creatures and creations in which I once implicitly believed are being proved by hard facts to be only figments of the imagination.  First I hear laughs when speaking of an actual living Robinson Crusoe ; then they say the beautiful story of William Tell has but a legendary foundation, that Gesler did not command Tell to shoot an apple off his son's head because there were no apples in Switzerland at that time.  Then magazinists worry one another with their everlasting gibberish, as to whether Bacon wrote Shakespeare or *vice versa*, and if so, whether Shakespeare ever lived.  About the same time intelligence comes to me which naturally changes my whole future —the distance of the sun from the earth, so long estimated at 92,960,000 miles, has been reduced by late measurement to the contemptible figure of 92,600,000.  But now I undergo the saddest disillusion of all.  The great maelstrom which whirls between two of the Loffoden islands never sucked down in its spiral abyss huge leviathans, nor three-deck frigates, firing broadsides, and with colors flying.  It is Edgar A. Poe, in this instance, who has so shamefully imposed upon my cheery credulity.  Even the geographies have only been romances.  Where will it all end?  When shall we know anything for a certainty ?

The maelstrom is simply a current between two

islands. Its swiftness depends almost entirely upon
the state of the wind and tide. There is at no time a
vortex and the fishermen actually drop their nets in
the centre of the channel. There is, however, some danger of a ship being driven upon the rocks when the
wind blows strongly from the northwest and meets the
tide with the immense body of water which is forced
into the narrow channel, so much more shallow than
the sea outside the islands to the west. There are
many like currents among the Loffodens, and all are
caused by similar pressure of outside sea upon straitened and shallow channels. Though ships are seldom
if ever driven aground, whales frequently are. As I
have said, the contracted entrances which are quite
deep outside, suddenly shoal within, and the generally
wary cetacean mammoth having incautiously entered,
it is impossible for him to retreat owing to the large
space required for turning his unwieldy body, and so
with the falling tide he is generally stranded and thus
becomes an easy prey.

The coast scenery in the neighborhood of the Loffodens is strikingly Alpine in character. As the reader
may already have gathered from my attempted descriptions, the scenery of Norway abounds in the most sudden and surprising contrasts. Changes of latitude
seem to effect nothing. Nature loves antitheses, and
we have Arctic scenes in the south, and almost tropical
scenery in the north. In the summer there is a north
wind and in the winter a south wind. It is a land of
contradictions. From the Loffodens to North Cape

snow falls occasionally during the summer months, and
though there is much fog and mist, there are no gales.
In winter, however, very heavy tempests rage along the
coast. These are frequently attended with lightning
which does much damage to the churches. It is even
said that as many as forty of these have been struck
and destroyed within the past fifty years. Deity does
not resemble the devil in taking care of his own.

The climate is, however, on the whole remarkably
mild. The temperature of the west coast is 20° higher
than corresponding latitudes in other countries. In no
other part of the globe do we find so great a surplus of
heat as that provided for Norway by the Gulf Stream.
Its influence is felt even as far as the frontier of Russia.
But for it Scandinavia would have a climate as rigorous
as that of Greenland, and would therefore not be a fit
abode for civilized beings. The manner in which the
industrious Gulf Stream does so much of the work of
the laggard winter sun is worthy of explanation and
praise. For a long distance out into the ocean along
the entire coast of Norway, extend huge shelving banks
which render the water there comparatively shallow,
and the great warm current flowing steadily over these
banks is thus in a measure prevented from parting with
its heat below, while the copious supply of vapor it en-
genders is carried by the winds over the whole country
and condensed into clouds which thus serve as a barrier
against loss of heat upwards by radiation. The store
of heat accumulated in the ocean's depths and continually replenished in the tropics is so enormous that

the most rigorous of northern winters fails to exhaust it. Thus at North Cape, which is in latitude 71 degrees 11 minutes north, the sea never freezes. And although the difference in latitude between it and Christiania is over 12 degrees, their temperature during the winter months is the same.

In Siberia agriculture ceases at 60 degrees of north latitude, but in Norway oats ripen under 69, rye under 69.30, and barley under 70. In Finmark the summer heat is intense, and daylight is continuous for ten weeks. The assistance of the Gulf Stream, so much appreciated in winter, may then well be spared. The rapid growth of vegetation is almost incredible. During this season crops are sown, ripened, and reaped. It has been found by experiment that in latitude 65 degrees north, barley will grow two-and-one-half inches and peas three inches in the twenty-four hours for several consecutive days! Barley is harvested in ten weeks after being sown. At Hammerfest, in latitude 70.40 north, the grass grows underneath the snow, and hay is made in a month after the snow has left the fields. Here the Scotch fir flourishes vigorously, sometimes reaching an altitude of eighty feet. But a little further east in this same latitude, in winter, mercury and even brandy frequently freeze in the open air.

A Norwegian scientist, Dr. Schubeler, has been engaged in making experiments during the past thirty years to determine the effects of the midnight sun, during the Scandinavian summers, on the wheat and other grain crops. The conclusion he draws is that wheat, corn and other seeds imported from a warmer clime, when cultivated under this unintermittent sunlight, become hardier as well as larger, and better able to resist excessive cold. The colors of these grains are also gradually changed to a richer and darker hue. These are not, however, the only variations that plants undergo by exposure to a night and day sun. The aroma and flavor of wild and cultivated fruits, capable of ripening in northern lands, are much more perceptible by the senses than are the aroma and flavor of fruits grown under more southern skies. This is particularly observable, Dr. Schubeler says, in the small fruits which are so grateful in the early part of the warm season. The experiments of this Norwegian scientist derive double interest from the recent inquiries of Dr. Siemens, illustrating the power of the electric light when applied to plants and vegetables to quicken and invigorate their growth. Both investigations, though entirely independent, have led to the same scientific result.

# CHAPTER IX.

## Farthest Thule.

The islands of the west coast of Norway, within the Arctic Circle, are frequented by eider-ducks, and whole flocks of them fearlessly swirled, in air and water, about the steamer as we swiftly pursued our course. These ducks are nearly the size of the common goose. Although their flesh is quite palatable, they are never killed, because the feathers with which they line their nests supply the well-known and valuable eider-down of commerce. Their nests, composed of marine plants and built upon the ground, are lined with small, soft feathers which the female plucks from her own body. When she has stripped herself of all her down, the male furnishes his. The birds will allow their nests to be robbed of feathers three times, after which they desert the locality. A nest will produce about half a pound of down, which, when picked and cleaned, is reduced one-half in weight. This down is so elastic that an amount which may be compressed between the hands will serve to stuff an entire coverlet! The weight of this will scarcely be perceptible, but it will prove warmer than the finest blanket. I am told that if the feathers are plucked from the breast of a bird which is dead they will possess no elasticity.

We called at several small fishing stations in the Loffodens, and then the next important stoppage was at Tromsoe, the capital of a province of like name which contains about 50,000 inhabitants—Norwegians, Lapps, and Quains. There are many relics of antiquity in this province, as in Nordland. In one place is an immense heap of reindeer horns and bones, deep in the midst of which human remains have been discovered. Here long ago the Lapps probably sacrificed to their divinities. Cairns of earth and stone are frequently met with in the interior. These have usually a hollow chamber which doubtless once contained an idol. In one of them, at least, a gigantic block of stone representing a Lapp deity has been found. Both on the sea-shore and in the valleys, caves have been discovered which contained human bones. Stone barrows also abound. There is only one large town in this province—Tromsoe.

The scenery from the Arctic Circle to Tromsoe is simply superb. Such a moving panorama is to be had nowhere else in the world. The traveler has but to comfortably seat himself upon the deck of the passing steamer and gaze, wonder, and admire. Thus is he ecstatically regaled without the slightest personal exertion or harassment. This part of Norway, were its merits properly made known, would, I feel sure, soon rival Switzerland as a vacation-ground for the overworked, and all in search of the grand and picturesque in nature.

Tromsoe lies upon the sloping sides of a low, verdant

island. Fish warehouses four stories in height line the
fiord. The streets are broad and run at right angles.
There is not a large assortment of stores. I counted
eight watchmakers in a walk of ten minutes. It being
daylight during the greater part of the summer, and in
winter very dark during all the twenty-four hours, save
from 10 A. M. to 2 P. M., I do not wonder the townsfolk
need so much assistance in enabling them to keep the
run of time. There is, however, a general atmosphere
of thrift and business that is quite astonishing in a place
situated so far within the septentrional regions. Tromsoe was founded over eighty years ago, and contains at
present about 5,000 inhabitants. It has a high-school
and seminary, three banks and a museum.

From Tromsoe we go on to Hammerfest, the most
northerly town in Norway and in the world, unless we
are to dignify the few huts of Upernavik, in Greenland,
by the name of town. But that may doubtless claim
title as the remotest boundary of semi-civilized existence. Hammerfest is situated upon the western side
of a little island called Kvalo. There is not a tree or
bush in sight anywhere. The town and surrounding
hills have an incomparably dreary appearance. It is
said the island was at one time well wooded, but the
trees have all been cut down for domestic use and no
young ones have been planted in their places. Fortunately for the inhabitants, much drift wood is brought
hither by the Gulf Stream. "Think," says Taylor, "of
Arctic fishers burning upon their hearths the palms of
Hayti, the mahogany of Honduras, and the precious

woods of the Amazon and Orinoco." But thus the
Equator communicates her sympathy to the Pole.

Hammerfest is simply a collection of tumble-down
warehouses and dwellings bordering the base of a rocky
cliff and extending along a narrow peninsula that makes
a natural breakwater behind which lie perhaps thirty
small vessels. Many of these are Russian traders which
bring wheat and corn from Archangel, on the White
Sea. It is customary also for many sloops, of from
twenty to forty tons burden, to leave here annually, in
the month of May, for the island of Spitzbergen, about
four hundred miles distant to the northward, where their
crews gather eider-down and hunt white bears and
walruses. Hammerfest is over a hundred years old.
At present it contains about 2,000 inhabitants. Its
trade consists in the purchase and reshipment of the
Finmark fisheries, the manufacture and export of cod-
liver oil, the fitting-out of expeditions to the fishing-
banks, and occasionally of one to the Polar regions.
Two weekly newspapers are published in Hammerfest.
It must be a rather dreary place during the long winter,
notwithstanding the fact that the people are then very
gay, and that balls and dinner-parties and other amusements are quite common. The revels at a wedding
feast, it is said, are sometimes continued for three
weeks, or until every person becomes exhausted with
excitement and dancing.

I found on the skirts of the town a most comfortable and cheery little inn, kept by a Norwegian woman
who did everything possible for my comfort. Ham-

merfest seems to consist chiefly of one long street which extends around the bay. It is a sort of raised stone causeway with a narrow sidewalk and deep ditches on each side. Most of the houses which border it are made of logs, and have very diminutive doors and windows. In one extremity of the town are several hovels, with walls six feet in thickness and made of loose stones and turf, which resemble those one frequently sees in Ireland. These are inhabited by poor Norwegian fishermen.

The odor of cod-liver oil fills half the town. I visited one of the factories where this valuable secretion is made ready for exportation. There was no necessity to inquire the way; the sense of smell directed. It is well that those for whom the oil is medically prescribed, do not witness the processes of manufacture. For myself, I should prefer having a little consumption—not too much, of course—rather than swallow any of this nauseous remedy. In a shed by the side of the harbor were huge vats filled with the livers of the cod-fish, and the oil which rises to the surface is skimmed off and put into huge copper kettles to be boiled. Six of these kettles are arranged around furnaces in which fierce fires were raging, and men begrimed with oil and dirt stood about stirring the cauldrons with enormous spoons. There are second and third rate qualities obtained by boiling the refuse, and these are employed in dressing and currying leather and serve also for lamp oil. In an adjoining shed stood many of the barrels, prepared for shipment. One of the men thoughtfully brought me a glass of the clarified oil to taste, but what with the surrounding sights and smells my gustatory nerves protested, and I was obliged to decline the insidious attention.

To abruptly change the subject from a dangerously sick man's diet to that of a remarkably well man : for dinner, so many miles within the Arctic Circle, my landlady gave me—give ear, O, ye gourmets!—trout; reindeer-tongues and string beans; stewed hare and potatoes; wheaten cakes; and a delicious small fruit, of which I do not remember the name. It resembles somewhat a cranberry, though it is eaten with cream and sugar. This dainty repast was moistened throughout with rich spicy beer and was consummated with a little glass of strong native brandy, followed by the calumet. As I was concluding, a man under the window blew a few notes on a bugle and then read aloud a notice to the effect that a certain steamer would leave that night for a certain place provided a certain number of people signified a desire to become passengers. He then departed for another part of the town to test his lungs and his hearers' ears in like manner. So you see that the vocation of the public crier has not yet become extinct —at least in the far north of Norway.

It seemed rather absurd to go to bed with perfect daylight at half an hour after midnight, but one must needs sleep sometime. A large stove in my room produced a very comfortable feeling, but I could not honestly say as much for a bed but five feet in length. The proprietress had apparently appreciated my eagerness to obtain latitude, and had supposed that longitude was, for the time, altogether out of my calculations. However, by removing the bolster and wedge-shaped cushions which one finds throughout Scandinavia as well as Germany, and by doubling up my pillow a little and myself very much, I succeeded finally in getting to bed. Though there was but a sheet and coverlet over me, I slept both warm and well, for the coverlet was stuffed with the heat-immuring eider-down.

Upon going forth in the morning, I perceive that on a long rocky peninsula across the harbor of Hammerfest, stands a small granite column, which is surmounted by a bronze terrestrial globe. An inscription in Latin and Norwegian states that this is the most important station, the septentrional terminus, of the great European arc of meridian 25° 20′, of which the southern extremity is on the Danube. This was also one of a chain of stations extending from the equator to the pole, for making pendulum observations in order to learn the variations of gravity on the earth's surface. The column was erected by the sovereigns of Norway and Sweden, and Russia.

I have never seen so many nor such enormous stingers or jelly-fish (*Cyanea capillata*) as there are in these northern waters. They are frequently a foot in diameter, with great masses of fibrous tentacles streaming after them in the sea, like the tail of a comet. Occasionally they expose a portion of their gelatinous surface above the water. They swim alongside of the steamer, alternately opening and shutting themselves

as we do an umbrella. They were in search of such
food as may have been thrown overboard. But since
they have no cerebrum, it is difficult to believe they
possess so much intuition as this action would seem to
imply—that is, supposing it is possible for instinct to
exist without brains, a theory which has not yet been
proven. I sometimes distinctly saw enveloped in the
transparent jelly, of which the bodies of these curious
connecting links between the vegetable and animal
kingdoms seem composed, full-grown, five-rayed star-
fish. How they manage to digest them it is difficult
to conceive.

Sometimes the jelly-fish drift near the surface of
the water, their mushroom-shaped disks uppermost;
again, they draw themselves along, several feet below the surface, with their ribbon-like fringes reaching upwards, as if hoping thus to entangle prey without being seen themselves. They expand at first
into distinct and perfect-shaped stars, then the points
seem to melt into a smooth edge as they contract close
around the spongy roots of the tentacles. Stingers
consist of nothing but stomach, and their sole mission
in life seems to be to skirmish around and fill it. They
are the gourmands of the sea. How long they exist,
how many children they have, whether they enjoy life,
these and a few kindred questions one would very
much like to have answered. But they are resolutely
reticent on all these points: uncouth and uncomplain-
ing they drift gently along with the tide, lie complacently by the side of the steamer, and silently and gin-

gerly take to their arms the sedate but succulent star-
fish. Alas, it is the caress of death to the poor little
radiate.

One of the weekly papers of Hammerfest is styled
the "Finmark Post." It is a single sheet of four
pages and twelve columns, and about a foot square.
It contains chiefly articles copied from French and
English journals, and local items and advertisements,
though there are telegrams from the capitals of the
world whenever there is news of great importance. In
a number which now lies before me, there is an article
of a column and a half, which discusses the relative
merits of Disraeli as novelist and statesman. A column
is devoted to the timber interests of the province, another to the shipping ; a brief paper considers the state
of the foreign fish market, and a few paragraphs gently
upbraid the nation for the money sent out of the country in support of the Hamburg lottery. The remainder
of this, the most northerly newspaper of the world, is
taken up with advertisements of steamers and trading-
ships. The "Finmark Post" is printed in the Norsk
character, and sells for the equivalent in our coinage
of four cents a copy.

But perhaps the reader is growing impatient to learn
more in detail my impressions of this people and country. These I have purposely delayed giving heretofore,
partly in order not to interrupt too much the narrative
of the journey, but rather, in imitation of the judges in
the courts, that I might be continually receiving evidence from every quarter, until, when about to leave

the kingdom, decision might appropriately be pronounced. I will therefore now devote a chapter to a consideration of the characteristic traits of Norway and the Norwegians.

# CHAPTER X.

## COUNTRY, CHARACTER, AND CUSTOMS.

NORWAY, as the reader is aware, constitutes about one-half of the great Scandinavian peninsula. It is a little over 1,000 miles in length, and from 40 to 275 miles in breadth. A great chain of mountains, with numerous branches, runs through its entire length. Nine-tenths of its surface consist of high plateaus and one-thirty-eighth of it is covered by perpetual snow. There are few navigable rivers, owing to the numerous rapids and falls. The country is for the most part cut up into deep narrow valleys, which are very thinly settled. The towns are small and separated by much mountain wilderness. Only three of them in the whole kingdom,—Christiania, Bergen, and Trondjhem— have more than 20,000 inhabitants each. Whenever you meet with a dozen farmhouses, a church and a couple of stores, there, in Norwegian comprehension, exists a town.

The ancient moraines, remains of a more Arctic fauna, giant pots, shell banks, sand terraces, and strand lines make Norway a very interesting country for the palæontologist and geologist. Fossils, however, are not available as a means of livelihood for the people, who must seek their support either on or in the ground—the primal source of the wealth of all nations. Minerals are indeed found in this country, iron, copper, silver, nickel and cobalt, but none of the mines are very productive, and coal to smelt the ores must be imported from abroad at a high price. So the great mass of the people cannot live by means of what is found in the earth. Nor can they all live by what is on its surface. There are only two comparatively level tracts in the country, those around Christiania and Trondjhem. Here the soil is extremely fertile and produces freely. But the remainder of Norway may be said, in brief, to consist of rock and snow, not more than 140 square miles of its entire area being under the plough.

A great scourge to Norway are the lemmings, which sometimes visit it in great numbers, and devour all the corn and herbage in their track. The Norwegians, it is said, once had a lemming-litany in their church service, in which these pests were most solemnly exorcised! The lemmings are of nearly the same size and appearance as a water-rat. They come in immense multitudes about once in four years. They are attacked immediately by various birds of prey, such as owls, buzzards, and hawks. Even the reindeer does not disdain to help in the task, and kills them by a stroke of its hoof, eating only the stomach. The Norwegians imagine that the presence of the lemming betokens a severe winter, but it is more probable that too great increase of numbers produces a scarcity of food, for which they therefore go in search. They travel always in a straight line from east to west, swimming the rivers and fiords until they reach the islands off the coast, and the sea, where multitudes are drowned. They move chiefly at night. The survivors never return eastwards, This is explained doubtless by the fact of so many relentless enemies pursuing them.

If it were not for the fish from the adjoining sea, and for the forests which cover four-fifths of the surface of Norway, the people would starve. The fishing interest has been already discussed. The valuable woods which are exported are pine and fir. These are cut in the forests in winter and dragged to the nearest river and placed upon the ice. When this breaks up in the spring, they are carried down by water to the fiord or seaside, ready for exportation. The timber is sent chiefly to England, France and Holland.

Notwithstanding the fact that the soil is shallow and that the winter lasts through seven months of the year, still I could plainly see, during my journey across the country from Christiania to the west coast, that the peasant farmers owed their extreme poverty largely to themselves. Their farm implements are most antiquated and rude, and they till the ground exactly as their forefathers did centuries ago. Potatoes grow in all parts of Norway. They were introduced in 1770, through the instrumentality of a sister of George III. of England, and are always to be found at every farmhouse But though cabbages, turnips, carrots, onions, and peas will grow in almost all sections, they are seldom seen at table. In winter you cannot get any green vegetables anywhere. The southern part of the country is capable of producing many delicious fruits, though gooseberries and strawberries are all I remember having eaten. Very little wheat is grown. Breeding horses and cattle would be a profitable occupation were it pursued as it should be. As in Denmark, the land is mostly held in very small farms. There are no great landowners and no laws governing the transmission of property as in England. The farmers are quite content to live in log-houses with grass roofs, and to allow their women to do much of the drudgery. Cleanliness is not nearly so general as it might be, and domestic economy is quite in its infancy. The lot of peasant and proprietor is much the same. Few people are rich, save possibly some of the traders and ship-owners.

If in any sense it were justifiable to compare Norway with the United States, I could but style it a very "slow" country. The people do not lack intelligence, but they certainly are wanting in ambition, energy, enterprise and business tact. In many places where the peasants seemed to be greatly suffering from poverty and their alleged inability to get a decent living from the soil, I suggested to them the feasibility of vastly increasing the facilities for reaching the wonderful landscapes of the interior, of building comfortable hotels, of making tracks through the forests to famous waterfalls, and of furnishing better classes of vehicles for traversing the rough mountain roads ; for all of which travellers would be only too glad to pay, and which would serve at the same time to greatly increase the amount of foreign travel to the country. It seemed quite a new thought to them. They had fish and potatoes to eat, a log hut with one room for a family of a dozen to live in, and homespun clothes which were warm enough for winter and could be exactly graded to the variations of summer temperature by the simple process of removing piece after piece. Why trouble themselves? No, indeed, the foreigners who were funny enough, or crazy enough, to scramble over ten miles of rough rock to see a simple stream of water running over a precipice because it had to go somewhere ; the tourist who was anxious to drive through a hundred miles of dirt and dust merely to be able to stand at last in the midst of a green valley or at the foot of a mountain glacier, might continue to do so, without any of the luxuries of travel, for all they cared.

It is a comfortable thing for these peasants that there are no heavy taxes in Norway, and that such as exist fall upon the importers, the rich, and not the poor. The protective duties are high but still native manufactures do not seem to make any headway. The difficulty of obtaining a livelihood at home drives many of the Norwegians to the United States. Thus in 1869, 18,000 emigrated hither ; in 1872, 15.000 ; and in 1873, 10,000. Since the latter year emigration has been gradually falling off, having had an annual range of from only 3,000 to 5,000. The men work for the most part as farm-hands, the women find employment in the dairies. They go generally, as I have said in the Preface, to the Western States—to Minnesota, Illinois,

Wisconsin, and Iowa.   A comparatively few settle in
Massachusetts.   They never return to Norway save on
short visits to their relatives.   Often they are not only
too poor to emigrate to another country, but even to
seek out better portions of their own land.   I asked
some of the people living at the base of a mountain on
the Hardanger fiord why they did not go to the more
fertile districts about Christiania or Trondjhem, and
they replied that they were too poor to pay the trifling
cost of moving, to say nothing of being able to purchase
a farm when they reached their destination.

The Norwegians are a tall, hardy, long-lived race.
They are simple, hospitable, patriotic and religious.
Their features have a strong tendency to the German
type.   Many of the women are quite pretty and the
children especially so, though the severe climate, or a
toilsome life, or a general ignorance of hygiene, tends
soon to deprive them of their bloom.   Education is
almost compulsory, from the fact that the clergy will
confirm no one until he has had a certain amount of
schooling, and such confirmation is a very desirable
means of preferment in public and private life.   It is,
therefore, difficult to find any who cannot read, write,
and cipher.   The Norwegians are also generally an
honest, sober, law-abiding people.   It is proved by
statistics that Norway is the only country in Europe in
which the number of suicides is not increasing.   This
fact is attributed to the stringent regulations against
drunkenness which are in force there ; for this loath-
some vice everywhere causes from thirty to forty per

cent of the suicides which prevail. Murders are almost unknown. The special punishment allotted to this crime by the criminal code, though very rarely enforced, is that of decapitation with a sword, as in China, Japan, and Morocco.

The Norwegian houses, mostly built of wood, save in the large towns, are often very attractive in their interiors. They are furnished as a rule quite plainly, with but few chattels, and before the pretty lace curtains of many sitting-room windows one often sees, from the street, banks of beautiful flowers neatly arranged in porcelain pots. The floors are either bare or covered with oil-cloth. Looking-glasses are common, though small. Beds are merely short and narrow boxes—just about large enough for the doubled-up body of a Peruvian mummy. The ceilings, which are at the same time the floors of the room overhead, render all words spoken and all movements made above distinctly heard below. The walls are often made of simple canvas, painted. This people seem to have no knowledge of ventilation. In fact, they have a morbid dread of fresh air. Scarcely any provision is made for its admittance into their churches, theatres, houses, or steamers. And like the Germans and Russians, eight or more persons, all smoking, will sit, on a cold night, in the compartment of a railway carriage with the windows entirely closed. On a steamer I have been one of sixteen persons who slept in a small cabin, the door and windows of which were all tightly shut, except a single "bull's-eye" not more than six inches in diameter.

Though the Norwegians surpass the Icelanders, with whom there is some propriety in contrasting them, in the comfort of their dwellings, in dress they are rather behind them. The clothes of both men and women suggest the style of a century ago. None of them fit, and the contrast of colors is most amusing. In many of the distantly-rural parts you sometimes, though rarely nowadays, see the picturesque costumes of the peasantry. This class of the people, for the most part, make their own clothing and shoes. Their wants are very few and they buy nothing that they can possibly manufacture in their houses or produce on their lands.

In Norway no special degree of respect is shown the women. They are generally left to shift for themselves, and this they are not slow in doing, naturally to their own advantage. Like the Danes, the Norwegians are extravagantly polite to each other in the streets. They are continually removing and replacing their hats. In a small town where one meets one's acquaintances perhaps a dozen times a day, you may imagine what a nuisance this custom becomes. Spitting, and without the provocation of either pipe, cigar, chewing tobacco, or even influenza, is a national bad habit. Like that of the American repeating voters, early and often seems to be their motto. I have seen persons spit upon the floor before company in their own parlors. On the steamers, though the sea is so convenient, the deck is generally covered with spittle. The spittoon is a domestic article quite unknown. The genius for expectoration is certainly not limited to the United States politician.

The Norwegians are not epicures, nor even what might be termed good livers. They have but little variety on their tables; the food is not always of good quality; and even if the original material is good, it is pretty certain to be spoiled in the cooking. The Norwegian manner of preparing and dressing victuals I must emphasize as especially bad. Fish and potatoes may be called the staple diet of the whole country. A cup of coffee is usually taken upon rising in the morning. Then at nine o'clock comes breakfast. This meal is usually preceded by a very small glass of brandy, flavored with caraway seeds. Upon the table are many small dishes of cold ham, tongue, sausage, anchovies, sardines, and several kinds of cheese. Sometimes these dishes are served upon a sideboard, to which periodical visits from the table are made. Then some warm fish and potatoes are brought in. These are ravenously attacked, and next the cold dishes are apt to be pounced upon again, and the most outrageous dietetical crimes are unblushingly perpetrated. Beefsteaks and mutton-chops are rarely seen. Dinner is usually served at two o'clock. It consists of soup, fish, meat and pudding; there is rarely any fruit, save a kind of pickled currant, which is eaten with the meat. Good beer, and claret which is rarely good, are the popular drinks. Upon rising from the table it is etiquette to say something (in Norsk, of course,) to the effect that you have made a good meal—how often a gastronomic perjury!—bow-

ing at the same time right and left, and to your *vis-à-vis*
This recalls the pretty and graceful table-benediction,
"Gesegnete Mahlzeit" (May the meal be blessed to
you), which one hears all over Germany. Supper is
ready at eight or nine. Like breakfast, it is begun with
a small glass of aquavit, followed generally with beer,
though sometimes with tea. The supper table resembles the breakfast table, except in the species of the
genus cheese. Thus I have frequently seen six varieties of coagulated curd on the table at the same time,
one or two of them being quite good, but several native
kinds rank and more distasteful to an American palate
than the reindeer cheese of the Laplanders. Many
gentlemen take a glass of hot brandy-toddy before
retiring for the night.

Table manners are at a low ebb in Norway. Con-
sistency does not seem to be regarded as a jewel. The
same people who bow so very ceremoniously to each
other and express sympathy and interest in the veriest
trifles of life, and who dance and grimace fully five
minutes at an open door before they can determine
which shall enter first, are exceedingly ill-bred during
meal time. Their knives wander so far down their
throats that one must at least admire their courage,
though failing to appreciate its object. In these feats
they rival the professional knife-swallowers of Bombay.
They hold their forks like pens. Even a four-tined
fork is not considered too unwieldy to use as a tooth-
pick. All knives are put promiscuously into the butter
dish, which indeed is never provided with a separate

implement. Also when spoons are furnished a public
dish, a Norwegian generally prefers using his own.
Eggs are sucked from the shells. The people eat most
voraciously, displaying the appetites of tigers, and making disagreeable noises with their mouths. They rise
and reach across the table for something you could
readily pass to them, and sometimes a person gets up
and walks to the end of the table for some particular
dish he fancies. When the plates are changed at the
end of a course, the knives and forks are apt to be
simply wiped by the waiter upon a towel in full sight,
and then complacently returned to you. And yet it
was the Scandinavians who won from Voltaire the
praise of being the "Frenchmen of the North," on
account of their punctilious politeness. Kind-hearted
and well-meaning, but surely somewhat deluded old
man !

It is always difficult to characterize at one and the
same time the national traits of an entire people. The
foregoing remarks, therefore, may be understood to
apply rather to the middling classes, the well-to-do
gentlemen—merchants, farmers, and government officials—whom the foreigner is most apt to encounter in
the hotels, on the steamers and cars, and occasionally
in private houses during his travels about the country.
Of course the refined gentleman is hardly the less so,
whether you find him a native of the burning sands
of Arabia or of the wild fastnesses of South Africa.
Stanley says "the conduct of an Arab gentleman is
perfect," and Parker Gilmore writes that he found the

king of the Bechuanas "in every respect a gentleman—in appearance excessively well-bred, and in his language courteous and considerate." But certainly many of the Norwegians must have had good educations and been brought up in good society, or at least have associated long enough with foreigners to have learned to imitate more of their good qualities. In any event it is a significant fact—and in this connection I call to mind also the Spaniards — that people can be at one and the same time extremely polite and excessively vulgar.

The peculiar form of government of this nation was to me an interesting study. Norway is a limited constitutional monarchy. As far as the making of war or peace and the being represented at foreign courts, Norway and Sweden are one State, but in other respects they are two distinct sovereignties, quite independent of each other. Norway, in its constitution and methods of government, has always been more democratic than her neighbor. She is assimilated in feeling to our republic, while the government of the sister nation is rather of the English type. Norway has her own parliament called the Storthing, while the legislature of Sweden is termed the Diet. Norway has a national bank, and is only responsible for the debts which she herself may contract. The business of the government is divided into seven departments : the treasury, the home, the judicial, the navy and post, the war, the ecclesiastical, and the audit departments. The executive power is vested in the sovereign, whose full title is "King of Sweden and Norway, the Goths and Vandals."

The latter part of this title seems somewhat equivocal in the honor it conveys.

Apropos of royalty and rank, I may say that in Norway there is no nobility, no aristocratic class ; but in Sweden, owing to the prevalence of the German cus- tom that every count's son shall be a count, and every baron's son a baron, the nobility is not only very nu- merous but, singularly enough, also very proud and very poor. The multitude of titles is perfectly bewil- dering  Of the Swedish orders of knighthood that of the Seraphim is regarded as the highest, being bestowed only upon crowned heads and persons of the greatest distinction. It was recently and most worthily given to the renowned Swedish navigator, Nordenskiöld, about whom all the world has lately been talking. The deco- ration of the Polar Star is chiefly confined to men of science. There are four or five other orders, but they are so indiscriminately conferred as not to be held in any very great esteem. In this respect they resemble a well-known French order founded by the First Consul —a legion having as members only about 50,000 cheva- liers and 10,000 officers—and so frequently to be seen in the streets of Paris that a stranger would be almost justified in inquiring who the people without red rib- bons in their coat lapels were. In France, it may be mentioned, in passing, there are upwards of five hun- dred dukes ! But I believe the government does not even take into consideration the myriad of counts.

The Norwegian parliament consists of an upper and a lower house, corresponding somewhat to our

Senate and House of Representatives. At present there are about one hundred national representatives. These are not returned directly by those entitled to vote, but by certain electors, who are chosen for every town and parish by the resident voters. Suffrage is not universal in Norway. To enjoy the privilege of voting, you must be at least twenty-five years of age, must have lived five years in the kingdom, and must be living there at the time of the election. You must also possess or have farmed, for the space of five years, registered estate in the country ; or be the owner of house property in some town or village, of the value of $336 of our money. Any person thirty years of age, ten years resident of the kingdom, and a professor of the Lutheran faith, may be sent to the legislature. Only members of the Lutheran or State church are admitted to office. In this matter of belief, Norway resembles all European countries excepting England and France, where religious dissent is not a bar to political advancement. As soon as the session has commenced, in the month of February generally, the parliament elects one-quarter of its body as the Lagthing or Upper House. The functions of this assembly are deliberative and judicial. The remaining three-quarters constitute the Odolsthing or Lower House, in which all enactments are instituted.

Though the king has the power of veto, it appears that in using it he has recently made himself very unpopular. A bill requiring members of the Cabinet to attend the meetings of the parliament was passed four times and on each occasion by an overwhelming majority,

the king's veto to the contrary notwithstanding. The
latest news from Norway is to the effect that the Swedish and Norwegian press are excitedly discussing the
demands made by some of the Norwegians for the re-
peal of the act of Union and the establishment of a
Norwegian republic. The Swedish journals maintain
that the honor of Sweden is involved in this contest,
and that strong measures to maintain the integrity of
the Union should be employed if necessary. The rela-
tions between the king and the Norwegian parliament
are very strained, a large majority having denied his
right of final veto. The peasant farmers have a majority in the parliament, which in great part explains the
present condition of affairs. The Norwegian national
party desire to show that the supreme power rests with
the people, not with the king, who rules them by suffer-
ance.

Notwithstanding the political disagreements at home,
the foreign trade of Norway is increasing. At present,
in proportion to population, she has the largest commercial navy in the world. In 1878 the imports
amounted to about $47,500,000 and the exports were a
trifle over $30,000,000. Nickel is fast becoming a
noted export of the country. In 1875, fourteen mines
of this useful metal had been opened, and during that
year about 35,000 tons were shipped to foreign ports.

Though the population of Norway has doubled
since the beginning of the present century, it still numbers no more than 1,800,000, or less than the city of
Paris. The inhabited area is only 20 per cent of the

entire country.  There are but fourteen individuals to
the square mile, whereas in Great Britain there are
265 and in Belgium 469.  In Finland the rate is still
less than in Norway, in fact, it is the lowest of any
country in Europe, viz. 13 inhabitants to the square
mile.  The islands contain one-eighth, and the coast
region more than one-half of the total population of
Norway.  Nearly 15,000 people dwell at an elevation of
2,000 feet above the sea.

My impressions of the country, in brief, are that
though much of its superficial area is water and rock,
yet with a display of greater energy and enterprise, it
might be made vastly more productive in all its resources—animal, vegetable, and mineral.  The Norwegians are honorable and amiable, free from destruc-
tive passions and pernicious prejudices.  They have no
special bent of mind, no vaulting ambition to fire the
world, but are fond of a quiet, simple life, with kinsfolk
and friends, and home employments and enjoyments.

# CHAPTER XI.

## A Day at North Cape.

In going on to the northward from Hammerfest, the mountains, if not so lofty, become wilder and even more desolate looking. They are of a dull brown color and quite barren of vegetation. We passed a small island where the most northerly lighthouse on the globe guides the mariner on his voyage to the Polar Sea and welcomes him home again from its perilous experiences. As I have already said, the object of most travellers in going so far north is to obtain a sight of the sun shining at midnight. I was a few days too late to see it exactly at that hour, but as there was plenty of light all the evening, the presence of the sun would not have seemed at all remarkable. In this singular region of the earth the nights are illumined, so to speak, by the midnight sun in summer, and the aurora borealis in winter. Of these phenomena I was told the latter is, in its magic splendor, by far the most interesting. We have had no better description of the midnight sun than that given in his "Northern Travel" by Bayard Taylor, some twenty-five years ago.

The North Cape is the northern extremity of a ragged, star-shaped island called Mageroe, or Lean

Island. This is at least a very appropriate name, for it is a perfect picture of barrenness. Upon it, however, are a few animals—reindeer, hare, and ermine. On the eastern side also are one or two small fishing-stations of Norwegians and Lapps.

A never-to-be-forgotten day was that on which, my steamer having rounded the long and comparatively smooth headland of Knivskjaelodde, I saw before me the goal of my long journey, the North Cape of Europe —a huge mass of dark mica slate, with a perpendicular front scarred and weather-beaten by ages of storm. The rock is much too precipitous to be ascended on the western or northern sides, and so we double it, with feelings similar, I fancy, to those of Vasco de Gama when doubling the Cape of Good Hope. The steamer anchors in a little bight and we are rowed ashore in one of her boats. After a stiff climb of twenty minutes, we reach the plateau of the cape, about a thousand feet above the sea. The surface is bestrewn with small sandstones, mica slate, white quartz rocks, and coarse grass and moss. It is a very desolate region. Everything seems dead. We walk across the plain to the brink of the cliff. Here, defiantly facing the North Pole, a red granite column commemorating the present king's visit has been erected. Beneath a carved and gay-colored crown is an inscription in Norwegian, which simply states the fact that H. M. Oscar II. ascended "Nordkop" on the 2d of July, 1873. From this position the view to the south is closed by the higher parts of Mageroe ; on the west you see the sum-

mits of Hjelmesven and Rolfsven, and almost beneath
you, the long low promontory of Knivskjaelodde; to the
north lies the vast expanse of the Polar Sea, with not a
sail in sight; while to the east faintly appears on the
verge of the horizon the outline of the rocky peninsula
of Nordkyn, the most northerly point of continental
Europe, and strongly resembling North Cape in its
configuration.

It is a dark misty morning, throwing into bolder
relief the sombre cliffs around which sea-birds screech
and beating breakers awaken echoes long and loud.
My comrades have rejoined the steamer. Alone I sit
and look out, far out toward the Pole, as if I were
about to penetrate the secrets which it has guarded so
long and faithfully. I gaze upon the Arctic Ocean,
now so calm, but often, as the rocks below abundantly
testify, so majestic and awful, when lashed to fury by
the circumpolar tempests. Far off, as my chart indicates,
lies the island of Spitzbergen; and yonder, still farther
away, are the islands of Nova Zembla. I feel as if I
were now indeed upon the threshold of the unknown.
Such emotions rarely come, except to the most insatia-
ble nomad. A solemn stillness reigns upon the forbid-
ding cliff. There is no evidence of man anywhere.
There are no habitations, no tracks, no trees; naught
but rocks and moss and sand. I am

> "Alone, alone, all, all alone,
> Alone on a wide, wide sea."

The feeling becomes oppressive. A phantom influence,

like that proceeding from some mysterious and super-. natural being imprisoned within a tomb of ice, hovers around me.    Muffled voices, more or less than human, come breathing from those never-seen regions where frost rules absolute amid spectral splendors that we dream not of.

But no! I am not all alone, for our steamer is rounding the point and steaming towards the cliff.    We had received on board, at Hammerfest, an enterprising photographer, from Berlin, who was making a business tour through Norway.    That he might the better photograph the cape, our steamer moved around to the west side, where the most favorable view was to be had.    As she passed my position the steam-whistle was blown and the crew cheered.    I heard all most distinctly, though I was a long distance off and nearly a thousand feet above them.    It is doubtful if North Cape ever witnessed a more vigorous one-man-power attempt at noise than I perpetrated in return, though, as I afterwards learned, my phonetics were far less expressive than my frenzied pantomime.    I walked across the cape to its inland extremity, but found it all alike—a dreary wilderness of moss and stone, with an occasional morass.    Then having gathered some specimens of the lichen and rocks, and being successful also in discovering a few field flowerets for my herbarium, I returned down the steep cliff to the steamer, which had in the meanwhile come to the end of its artistic tour.    Later we breakfasted off some splendid large fish which one of the officers had caught during my absence.

The promontory of Knivskjaelodde, and not, as is generally believed, North Cape, is really the most northerly point of Norway and of Europe. It projects beyond North Cape at least half a mile, but as it lies low, while North Cape is high and prominent, the latter will perhaps always be called the most northerly headland. The translation of the name Knivskjaelodde is "knife-cut point," which pretty accurately describes its physical conformation. It is a sharp and narrow promontory about equally composed of battered and smoothed rocks. As we were so fortunate as to possess a photographer, I embraced the opportunity of having a picture taken of this point which should also include the captain, in addition to three passengers, of whom I was one. This was to be a souvenir of a visit very seldom if ever made before, as the sea is generally too rough, and the period of the steamer's stay too brief, to permit travelers to land, should they so desire. Besides, if the weather happened to be pleasant, it has always been customary to disembark upon the North Cape and upon that only.

After the photographer pronounces the negative satisfactory, we amuse ourselves by scrambling over the rocks to the uttermost limit of the promontory. It is quite low tide, and we crawl in eager rivalry over the slippery wet surface to the very margin of the water, and even there stretch out our legs and feet over the Arctic Ocean, poleward. It is an exciting contest, attended with some danger of a sudden cold and briny bath, but the author is successful at last, Nature having favored him with lengthier means of self-extension than his companions.    He is half inclined to flatter himself, therefore, that he has been farther north in Europe than any one else in the world.    But he wishes it distinctly understood that, "owing to a press of other business," he cannot at present accept any challenges.

Doubtless there are some sturdy solemn minds to whom all this may seem very foolish work, who may even wish to quote to me those lines of Isaac Watts upon "False Greatness," beginning

> "Were I so tall to reach the pole,
>   Or grasp the ocean with my span,
>   I must be measur'd by my soul :
>   The mind's the standard of the man."

I have not space here to argue this point, but these wretched detractors must at least admit that ours was a pleasing conceit, an innocent diversion that certainly added a spice to the more severe travel-study.    Another similar instance in my personal experience was on the watershed of the Rocky Mountains, at the sources of two rivers, where, having carried water from one stream to the other, I entertained myself with the thought of having thwarted Nature, by sending into the Pacific Ocean some water plainly intended for the Atlantic.

North Cape at a distance reminds me very much of Cape Horn, the southernmost point of South America, though this is in a latitude about twenty degrees further north, than that is south, of the Equator.    Both are

dark, rugged cliffs situated upon islands. Their difference in height is but little over two hundred feet.
Both are alike the homes of myriads of sea-birds. Both
are beaten upon by Polar winds and waves. And
though the route for vessels around Cape Horn is most
important, and of course most frequented, I think that
there will, before many years, be a steamer route around
North Cape to the mouth of the great Siberian River
Yenessei, and even to the Lena, which penetrate to the
borders of China, whose important trade will thus be
more readily secured for Europe and America. The
discoveries of Prof. Nordenskiöld hold out bright hopes
that such will be the case, for, during two months in the
autumn, the ice so far releases itself from the northern
coasts of Europe and Asia as to make this a practicable
route for steel steamers.

After waiting to see what steps, if any, the Scandinavian and Chinese governments intend taking in
furtherance of such a grand and important commercial
scheme, it is interesting to note that Russian strategists
are already profiting by Nordenskiöld's achievements.
The government has recently purchased in Sweden
three fast steamers, which are about to be dispatched
around Northern Europe and up the rivers Obi and
Irtish to Semipolatinsk, a town near the Russo-Chinese
frontier. By this expedient an enormous saving of time
and fatigue to the soldiery will be effected in conveying
reinforcements from Russia Proper to the extreme eastern limit of the Empire, whence a few forced marches
will bring them to the Chinese frontier, should the com-

plications still pending between Peking and St. Petersburg result in war.

North Cape and the surrounding headlands and fiords are said to yield a wondrous scene when irradiated by the golden gleams of the midnight sun. The brush of a Turner only, and not even the pen of a Taylor, could then do full justice to them. I thought of remaining over night on the grim old promontory, but the steamer having returned, it would then be necessary to walk a long distance to one of the fishing stations where a sailboat and men willing to take me back to Hammerfest would probably be found. The distance to the latter being nearly a hundred miles, the fear of contrary winds and heavy weather caused me reluctantly to renounce my intention. So we steamed away to the southwest, back from Nature's weird domain to man's bold aerie, while low-lying Knivskjaelodde rapidly faded from view. What a relief it was to quit such a scene of desolation! Thousands of sea-birds were crowded together upon some of the small islands. It is said that nearly every fowl of Northern Europe which preys upon sea-fish is to be found upon the coasts of Norway. But never a song bird is discovered; those delightful minstrels of the air seem unknown within the Arctic Circle.

We left upon the island of Maeso one of our passengers, a Norwegian surgeon, who was to be stationed at a fisherman's hospital there for three years. This hospital is supported by a tax on the province. There are 1,500 fishermen on that and the adjoining islands.

Maeso is a desolate enough looking place, with a few houses and a church. The lot of this surgeon is not to be envied, notwithstanding that his is the title of the "most northerly surgeon in the world."

At Hammerfest I rested a few days and then took another steamer south. It was one of the Hamburg-Vadso line, the regular mail line of the Norwegian coast. The steamer was built at Newcastle-on-Tyne. It was most comfortable in all its appointments, and the table was much better than that usually met with, though there was still left a considerable margin for improvement. We had a number of English gentlemen on board, among them the Earl of Dudley, who had been on a fishing excursion in his own steam-yacht far up in Northern Finland.

They have an ingenious method of getting as much as possible of the traveler's money on these Norwegian coasting-steamers. Thus : so much is paid down for a passage-ticket, which you afterwards discover calls only for a berth located probably in a small cabin where there are several other passengers. You also learn, probably · for the first time, that board will be extra. The option is given of arranging for a fixed price per meal, or if you are to be a passenger for more than three days, so much per day, generally $1,50 may be paid. This entitles you to breakfast, dinner, and supper, and seems reasonable enough, but when added during a long voyage, to a very substantial original passage-price, you discover that steamer-traveling in Norway is on the whole quite expensive.

I had intended to go only as far south as the town of Bodo. In traveling I make it a rule never to "double upon my track" when it can possibly be avoided, but in this instance it became absolutely necessary that the comparatively short distance between North Cape and Bodo should be remeasured. Had it been the winter season when sledges and reindeer could be employed, I should have gone from Hammerfest directly overland in a southerly direction to the Gulf of Bothnia. As it was I decided to travel from Bodo across Norway and Sweden to a town called Pitea, on the shores of a bay of like name. This would give me an opportunity to see a section of Scandinavia about as little known to Norwegians as to Europeans. For to my very numerous inquiries, the stereotyped replies always were, "there is no route across the country ; no one ever goes that way ; you will have to sleep in the forests ; you will get nothing to eat until you approach the Swedish Gulf ; you will find no horses, perhaps no suitable boats ; you will suffer from cold, wet, heat, mosquitoes," and so forth, *ad nauseam*. Such in truth was the doleful news that assailed my ears from the south to the north of Norway. But the prospect did not at all alarm me. I had heard in many parts of Asia very much worse accounts of interior districts that I wished to visit and had nevertheless successfully accomplished my purpose.

All travelers, it seems, who voyage to the North Cape, are accustomed to return by the same route the entire distance to Christiania, which, counting both ways, occupies about a month, passed on board a small steamer with its constant and unavoidable jar, jingle and jostle. The mere suggestion of varying the tour causes the average Norwegian to entertain serious doubts as to one's sanity. However, at last, I determined to go ahead, hoping, though of course not sure, that I was right—thus reversing the famous maxim of Mr. Davy Crockett. But before I ask the reader to accompany me on that little bit of exploration—for such it afterwards proved to be—I have much to say about the curious race of dwarfs who occupy the extreme northern parts of Scandinavia and Russia.

## CHAPTER XII.

### With the Lapps: By the Sea.

LAPLAND is the most northerly country in Europe.
It may be roughly said to comprehend all that region
lying between the Polar Ocean and the Arctic Circle,
and the Atlantic Ocean and the White Sea. Thus
about two-thirds of it belong to Russia, and the remaining portion to Sweden and Norway. The total area is
upwards of 150,000 square miles, a province nearly as
large as our State of California. In Lapland Nature
appears in a garb such as she wears nowhere else. But,
though situated so far north, it is not altogether a region
of snow, ice, and moss; nor is it, as many seem to imagine, a dreary, monotonous steppe, like Siberia. Lapland resembles Syria, in that its surface is generally
rocky and barren. But it is unlike Syria in certain
parts where the landscape is very beautiful, and diversified with fertile valleys, broad rivers, large lakes, and
dense forests. There is a body of fresh water in Finnish
Lapland more than double the size of Lake Champlain.
Its outlet forms part of the boundary line between Norway and Russia.

The summers are short, and, though very warm
during the day, are invariably cool and delicious at

night. The long twilight is an especially delightful period. Even Wordsworth, in one of his minor poems, can find no more vivid a comparison than "lovely as a Lapland night." The winters, however, are long and very severe. The interior and eastern parts are particularly cold at this season, the western coast being directly influenced by the comparatively warm Gulf Stream of the Atlantic. The limit of perpetual frost is 3,500 feet. The mean annual temperature of North Cape is thirty degrees above zero, reckoning by the scale of Fahrenheit.

In 1556, three years after the loss of Sir Hugh Willoughby, and one year before the death of Sebastian Cabot, son of one of the reputed discoverers of the continent of America, the master of an English pinnace named the Serchthrift, while making a voyage of discovery to the northward and eastward of Europe and Asia, called at the coast of Norway where the town of Vardohuus is now located. Near here he finds a land called Lappia, and its inhabitants, the Lappians are, he writes, "a wild people, which neither know God, nor yet good order: and these people live in tents made of deer-skins: and they have no certain habitations, but continue in herds and companies by one hundred or two hundred. And they are a people of small stature, and are clothed in deer's skins, and drink nothing but water, and eat no bread but flesh all raw." The remainder of the skipper's journal is taken up with what was doubtless of much greater importance in his eyes, namely, the commercial prospects of the voyage. This

brief sketch, however, taken three-and-a-quarter centuries ago, is the first account the English-speaking world
had of the existence of this pigmy race, and in all particulars, save their present bibulous propensity, is essen-
tially as true to-day as then.

It is a singular coincidence that Norway should produce at once the largest and the smallest men in Europe.
An American of average height, standing in a crowd of
Norwegians, would find so many as tall as himself or
taller, that it would be impossible for him to see over or
between their heads. In crowds of average-sized people
in other continental nations, the reverse of this would
be the case. The Lapps are of extremely low stature.
They average in height only four feet and a half ; one
five feet tall would be regarded as a prodigy in his own
land. Though owning a physical combination common
to both the Mongolian and Caucasian, I thought their
physiognomy possessed more of the characteristics of
the former race. Thus, in color they are yellowish-
brown, and they have large heads, with broad and low
foreheads, oblique black eyes, flat, short noses, broad
mouths, high cheek bones, scanty beards, and long, stiff
black hair. Their voices are not euphonious, being low
and squeaking. They possess great muscular power
and are extremely agile.

Ethnologists have been greatly puzzled as to the
origin of this strange race. Doubtless they entered
Europe before the historical period. Perhaps they were
the original inhabitants of Finland and were slowly
crowded north and west, around the northern extremity

of the Gulf of Bothnia, by the Finns. At any rate they appear to belong to the Finnic group of the great Turanian family. This opinion is based upon a consideration of their language, physique, features, and dress. The nomad character of the Lapps allies them to the Samoyedes and Esquimaux. In fact these three peoples, with certain less known tribes in Siberia, are classed together by some ethnologists as the Hyperborean Race. The word Samoyedes signifies "swamp-dwellers," referring to the fact of this tribe inhabiting the vast mossy plains of Northern Russia and Siberia. The name Esquimau means "eater of raw flesh," which appellation might, indeed, be bestowed with equal propriety upon all these circumpolar people. The Esquimau is the most widely spread nation in the world, though the highest expression of this type, as my readers doubtless know, is found in Greenland. Owing to the greater mildness of the climate of Lapland, the physical condition of her inhabitants is superior to that of the Samoyedes or the Esquimaux, though in mental and moral capacity perhaps the latter are the best endowed —at least they are the most adroit and teachable.

There seems to be some confusion in the designation of the different peoples of Norway. Thus, those whom we call Lapps are apt to be called Finns by the Norwegians, and those whom we have been accustomed to term Finns they characterize as Quains. The truth is that those who are styled Finns in Norway are really true Lapps. The Quains are properly the Finns of the northwest of Finland, that portion bordering on the

Gulf of Bothnia  The Lapps have, however, sometimes so nearly lost their original character as to be scarcely distinguishable from the Norwegian peasantry. In 1865, there were 4,000 people in Norway of mixed Finnish, Lappish, and Norsk blood. The descendants of such individuals, strange to say, are regarded as true Norwegians, which not only shows the readiness wherewith races are fused, but also indicates in a way, the rapidity with which the Laplanders are becoming extinguished.

The Lapp race is said to number at the present day only 17,000 souls. These are distributed in the various sections of Lapland as follows: Norway 5,000 ; Sweden 4,000 ; and Russia 8,000.  They are divided into two grand classes—the roving and the settled.  The former are called Boelappen or Mountain Lapps, and the latter Soelappen or Sea-Coast Lapps.  Those are herdsmen, and support themselves chiefly by hunting ; these live generally by fishing, rarely by tillage.  Originally all the Laplanders were nomadic, but the difficulty of finding sufficient food within the limited space to which the increasing civilization of the neighboring nations had gradually restricted them, has compelled many of the tribes to settle near the larger rivers and lakes, and more especially along the sea-coast. These Lapps, indeed, now largely outnumber those wandering over the hills and plains.  Villages are unknown among any of these people.  In the middle of the sixteenth century it might have been the custom of the Lappians to "continue in herds and companies by one hundred and two hundred," as stated on a preceding page, but nowadays an encampment contains only half a dozen tents or huts. In summer the lofty parts of the hills on the west coast of Norway, which cannot be utilized by the Norwegian farmers, are occupied by the vagrant Lapps. These bring their reindeer there for the moss-pasturage, and in order to avoid near the sea-shore, the attacks of insect pests, notably the gad-fly. Another and very important object of the Laplanders in going to the coast is, that they may dispose of the commodities they have collected during the winter, such as the skins of animals and the feathers of birds. These they usually barter for brandy, gunpowder, cloth, and meal. In the autumn they return with their herds to the great plains of the interior. It is estimated that more than 100,000 reindeer annually make these journeys with their Laplandish owners.

There are always many Sea-Lapps to be seen in Hammerfest. They go there from the surrounding islands to sell fish and reindeer venison, and to buy the few articles of foreign manufacture of which they appreciate the uses. They are especially fond of coffee and sugar, and the rye flour which comes from Russia. Some of them can read and write, having been instructed in these elementary helps to knowledge by Norwegian schoolmasters. Many Lapps are baptized when young ; and their weddings take place in the Norwegian churches. Nevertheless owing to their dirty habits and the national prejudice against them, they are not allowed to remain permanently in any of the towns while living, though, curiously enough, they may do so when dead. They are buried in the same cemeteries as the Norwegians, but no display is made at their funerals.

One night (though it was as light as day) while roaming over the wharves of Hammerfest I chanced to come upon a party of about twenty Sea-Lapps, engaged in bidding farewell to some friends who were returning to their homes on a distant part of the coast. There were several old women almost hideous in their ugliness, some smiling but homely girls, some young men and several children. One of the women had in her arms a little sickly-looking baby, which was exposed to the cold and rain and received no more attention from its mother than if it had been a bundle of reindeer moss. The whole party were dressed in pretty much the same style. The women wore long tunics made of fustian, ornamented with red and yellow borders, and confined at the waist by a belt. Their nether garments were of leather, as were their pointed shoes, which were tied about the ankle with colored straps. They wore a sort of woolen cap fitting tightly to the head and projecting above the crown somewhat like those one sees in Normandy, France. The men had cloaks of reindeer-skin, the fur worn within, and hoods of skin and wool. In winter they wear another suit over this, with the hair outwards. The boots they then wear are made of the skin of the reindeer's head (the toughest part of that animal), with the hair left on. The Lapps never wear linen or cotton undergarments. They are very fond of colors, which they employ in the brightest tints, but only a little is displayed at a time. This gives them an odd

but withal picturesque appearance. The natives who
were about to depart had come to Hammerfest in little
open boats; some fish, a birch-box of clothing and
another of provisions constituted their entire luggage.

While I stood gazing at these diminutive beings,
who, by the way, took not the slightest notice of me,
one of the hags produced a bottle of finkel, a vile native
brandy distilled from corn, which has been felicitously
described as "a mixture of turpentine, train oil, and
bad molasses." This was rapidly passed from mouth
to mouth, not excepting the women and young girls,
who actually rivalled the men in their alcoholic bibacity.
The liquor, which is almost strong enough to cauterize
the stomach of a European, caused some of the younger
members of the party to wince a trifle, but in a moment
they smiled again and were as merry as children at a
picnic. Indeed some of the men held their wives'
hands, swinging them, and laughing and talking in turn
with each person in the group. But soon the scene
changed, for the sad moment of separation came. The
women embraced and the men shook hands after our
own fashion. The children clung to their mothers.
Some of the girls even shed tears. The poor pale-
faced baby in its little skin cradle alone was impassive.
It was an intensely interesting scene : there, at midnight
in the outpost town of the civilized globe, alone with a
race of fellow-beings whose language, habits, faith and
thoughts I did not comprehend, but with whom I could
most heartily sympathize. "Verily," thought I, "though
we do not in a sense know each other, yet are we co-

members of the world's great family, and it will be my
own fault if we do not become better acquainted ere I
leave your secluded country." The little boats were
pushed off from the wharf, the men took their seats at
the oars, and the remainder of the party, without another word, turned and walked slowly back into the
town.

One day I attended a Lapponian wedding in the
church at Hammerfest. As I entered, the bride and
groom were standing before the altar; and about a
score of relatives and friends, the men on one side, the
women on the other, occupied the front seats. The
pastor in a black robe and white frilled collar, read the
service, and the sexton stood at the side, hymn-book in
hand, ready to lead the singing. The bride was attired
in a dark blue woolen tunic, with orange and red trim-
mings; her boots, fastened with a vari-colored ribbon
which was wound around them, extended half way to
the knee; over her shoulders she had thrown a small
gay-colored shawl. Upon her head she wore a brilliant
cap, with a huge bunch of narrow ribbons streaming
behind. The bridegroom was dressed in a similar style,
except that his tunic was shorter, and that he had upon
his head a simple woolen turban. The dress of the
female Lapps closely resembles that of the male. The
women all wear pantaloons, since open garments would
unnecessarily expose their bodies to the cold during
three-fourths of the year. Both sexes are, as I have
hinted, remarkably vain. In respect to dress or orna-
ment, whatever is gaudy is sure to be admired and cov-

eted. A white frock with edgings of red and blue is very popular. Oftentimes their holiday garments are gayly and handsomely embroidered.

The wedding-service, in Norwegian, is read, rehearsed, and sung by the pastor, with responses by the sexton. None of the Lapps seem to join in either the responses or the singing. At the close of the ceremony the pastor and sexton congratulate the enamored pair and, a procession being formed, the company march two by two, out of the church and down the street, to one of the large tenements provided for the Lapps by the merchants of Hammerfest. As the newly married couple pass me I notice that the bride is much the older and uglier. The bridegroom is a bright, cheery looking fellow, but a mere boy. Great heavens! could it be that even in distant Lapland they married for money? Upon inquiry afterwards I learned to my sorrow that such was indeed the fact. In this respect they are often worldly-minded, like their brothers and sisters of the west. However, they generally marry " for love," or rather for what is its nearest substitute in their comprehension. Byron tells us, and he certainly ought to have known, that

> " The cold in clime are cold in blood,
>   Their love can scarce deserve the name."

The Lapps are never divorced. A girl possessing property or money to the value of $50 would be styled rich. The dowry of parents to their daughters when they marry consists usually of reindeer, as many head as the condition of their finances will permit. A youth is often devoted to several girls at the same time—so unlike young Americans!—and he expresses his esteem by presents, chiefly of rings or other ornaments. If he marries one of them, all the others return him their presents. Could not this custom be introduced with advantage here? The Laplanders have no previous ceremony upon marriage occasions. After the church service, if there should be one, presents are interchanged and copious libations of brandy swallowed. The gifts consist of rings, spoons, silver cups, silk neckerchiefs, and sometimes, if the parties are very rich, silver girdles. The men marry at eighteen years of age, the women at fifteen. Polygamy is in vogue, and marriageable girls are often sold by their parents. The daughter of a rich man costs a hundred reindeer; that of a poor man about twenty. This price they consider as a repayment of the expenses incurred in bringing up a daughter, and also as a remuneration to the father for losing her services.

I joined the procession, and entering the house, was received with much respect and invited to join the nuptial party in their simple meal of boiled sheep. This I declined, but I could not do less than drink their health and happiness in a glass of nitro-glyc — no, I mean finkel; and afterward, I had the special pleasure of making the bride a present of a bright silver kroner fresh from the mint. She blushed crimson, while her husband endeavored to look as unconcerned as possible. The room into which I had been ushered was simple enough. It contained a couple of small tables, a few benches, and a pile of skins upon which several children were soundly sleeping. The Lapps when full-grown measure scarcely more than four feet in height, and their children being correspondingly diminutive are at all times interesting as curiosities. The company took with their hands great hunks of meat from a common dish, and having cut these into comparatively small pieces with the large knives they usually wear about their waists, they swallowed them at a gulp. The husband and wife were sitting side by side upon a box scarcely wide enough for one of them, and eating as voraciously and unconcernedly as if the happiest event of their lives served only to whet their appetites. Friends poured in, and the bottle of finkel poured out so rapidly, and I was persuaded by so many smiling men and chatty women to drink, that I thought best to beat a retreat, knowing they would all soon be drunk, and then nothing more of interest to me—or any one else for that matter—would be done. Dancing is unknown among the Laplanders, their only amusements seem to consist in drinking, eating, and hunting.

Passing one noon along the wharves, just as the fishermen were taking dinner, I was invited to join a grinning good-natured party in their boat. They had but two articles of diet—dried codfish and a chunk of seal-blubber about two feet square and three inches in thickness. These had been placed upon a wooden box, and the men were tearing and rending the codfish like lions feasting upon a buffalo, and ever and anon hacking off a tidbit of blubber which, having swallowed, they would roll up their little blue eyes and grin from ear to ear at me, as much as to say "don't we live well." The Lapps never cook either fish or blubber, but eat their "flesh all raw," an odd fact of which the sixteenth century traveller made special mention. My hosts washed down their piscatory provender with copious draughts from a large bottle of the stomach-stunning finkel. The codfish I found very dry and stringy, but not unpalatable. The seal-fat, however, I cannot say that I relished. It tastes exactly as whale oil smells. In fact, the seal oil of commerce is manufactured from this blubber. My portion was cut from the large Spitzbergen seal, but there is a small seal caught near Hammerfest, the flesh of which even Europeans do not despise, as its flavor much resembles veal. These Ichthyophagi generally support themselves by the cod-fishery, though occasionally they succeed in capturing a whale. This they do in a most singular manner. A harpoon being darted into the monster's body, is then broken close off. No more notice is taken of it at the time, but the wound usually proves mortal and in a few days the huge animal is probably found cast upon some part of the neighboring shore. The owner is known by a mark on the barb of the harpoon, and by this his property is identified. The law, however, entitles the finder to one-third of the booty.

Near this Lappish boat were many Russian trading-ships, which come to Hammerfest from Archangel, with very favorable winds, in four days. In rough weather

and with contrary winds, however, they are sometimes
a month on the way; though they generally manage to
insure themselves pleasant weather and quick passages
by making their voyages in the summer. Their trade
is very important for the poor Norwegians and the Laplanders dwelling on the northern and northwestern
coasts of Norway. The peasant classes of northern
Russia are but little above the Lapps in intelligence
and mode of life, and are even grosser feeders. Thus,
they eat a species of coarse fish which no Lapp will
touch and with which the latter supply them in exchange for rye flour. Putrid fish, bread once white
but turned black through acidity, and the worst kinds
of brandy, form the staple diet of the Russian sailors,
and on this they become unusually robust and strong.
In Hammerfest drunken Lapps and Russian sailors
reel through the streets together, but excite no com-
ment or even attention. It seems to be expected that
they should be in this condition about half the time.
Indeed, the besetting sin of these races, as of the Icelanders, is drunkenness. Another infatuation of the
Lapps, both male and female, is smoking. They always
carry a tobacco-pouch of reindeer-skin, and attached to
it a pipe-cleaner made of a bird's bill.

The powers of endurance of the Lapps are quite remarkable. They are naturally very sinewy and strong
and their exposed and intemperate life does not seem
to diminish their vigor, at least for a time ; though they
are apt to become prematurely old, still they manage to
linger on to very advanced ages. If overtaken by a

snow storm on the mountains, they simply allow themselves to be snowed in, and when the storm is over, dig
themselves out and proceed on their journey.   A Lapp
will get drunk, fall asleep in a snowdrift or a ditch and
awake in the morning as if in the warm room of a town
house.   In this wonderful display of vigor and vitality
they are excelled by no people within the limit of my
observation, save the Russian peasants.   Often in the
middle of winter a Lapp woman, during the wandering
of her people in search of moss for the reindeer, will
give birth to a child, and after a brief repose will continue the journey without any evil consequences.

Nature has not given the Laplander much of an
outfit.   Good-looking ones are like meteors ; they only
shine forth at rare intervals.   Still some of the younger
Lapps, in spite of their stunted figures, squinting eyes,
flat noses, and enormous mouths, present a comparatively handsome appearance.   But even this question-
able beauty disappears as they grow older.   I frequently
met Lapps in the streets of Hammerfest, man and wife
holding each other's hands, or the wife and children
clinging to the girdle of the husband.   This custom I
at first attributed to affection but afterwards concluded
it was indulged in solely with a view to greater comfort
in locomotion.   All have an ungainly walk, though
they are generally upright.   They are besides nearly
all of them more or less bow-legged, being allowed to
walk too early in life.   Other causes, however, which
tend to produce this physical defect, are riding in the
narrow pulkhas or winter sledges, the lowness of their

huts and tents, and their huge shoes which have no heels. The old women are especially ugly, and old people of this race meet with little if any sympathy from the young folks. Thus when the aged members of a travelling family or tribe fall sick upon the journey, they are provided with some victuals and left lying on the roadside, thus to fall a helpless prey to the prowling beasts of the vicinity.

## CHAPTER XIII.

### With the Lapps : On the Mountain.

Maupertuis, the French mathematician and astronomer whom Louis XV. sent to Lapland, in 1736, in order to determine whether the earth was pointed or oblate at the poles, by obtaining the exact measurement of a degree of longitude—a problem of great interest in those days—tells us in his work *De la Figure de la Terre*, that this remote country "everywhere presents subjects of reflection and contemplation : no arts flourish here; we nowhere meet with temples, houses, wrecks of columns, or of other monuments, but a fine opportunity is afforded of studying among the wandering tribes the first elements of social life; of society in its most ancient form." It was with such an object in view that while my steamer remained at Tromsoe on its upward passage, I eagerly embraced the chance offered of visiting some of the vagrant Laplanders—true gypsies of the North— who were at that time living in a neighboring valley.

Having procured a guide who spoke Lappish, we rowed across the fiord to the mainland and then walked up a dreary dale to the encampment. We first came upon two large circular stockades intended as a corral or pen for the reindeer, which at the time of our visit

were all away in the mountain pasture. We unceremoniously opened the door of the nearest hut and awoke
the sleepers within, for it was about two o'clock in the
morning. This very early call was necessary, for the
steamer was to leave at six, and as it was continually
light throughout the twenty-four hours I invariably went
on shore whenever there was anything of interest to be
seen, no matter what time of the night or morning it
might be. A very inharmonious chorus of dogs replied
to our greeting, but the Lapps having succeeded after
some delay in repressing them, we crawled—through a
door hung at such a slant that it closed of itself—into a
beehive-shaped hut, perhaps fifteen feet in diameter,
and eight feet in height, built of birch timbers which
were covered first with bark and then with turf and
stones. The whole interior was begrimed with smoke
whose only means of exit was a small square opening in
the centre of the roof, through which we looked up to
the sky. A large heap of skins was piled up on each
side, and nestling comfortably in the midst of them were
six or eight dogs. In the centre were the embers of a
fire, and above them a kettle was suspended from the
roof by a chain. On a shelf on one side were some
skins of cheese, a few fish, and a bowl of cream. The
food of these Mountain Lapps generally consists of the
soup and venison of the reindeer and the milk and
cheese of the same useful animal, but they will also eat
fish and rye flour when they can obtain them. On
another side were several birch boxes containing clothes
and books. At first, it seemed as if this was all that the

hut contained, but presently we saw a head peep from out one of the piles of skins, then another and another, and then others on the opposite side. It proved eventually to be a family of six—a mother, three girls, a boy, and a baby. The father, I understood, was absent in Tromsoe. Their birch-leaf beds were covered with seal-skins, their pillows were covered with sheep-skins, and they themselves were covered with reindeer-skins.

The old woman arose, put on her leather boots, filling them with hay, and then stood quite dressed before us. She wore a warm woolen undergarment, leather trousers, and a long leather tunic from which the hair was partially rubbed. On her head was a scarlet pear-shaped cloth cap. The woman could not be called handsome but had a good-natured smile. For a wonder she was not very inquisitive, desiring only to know my nationality and anxious to sell me something. I asked what there was to be sold and was shown several pairs of winter boots, lined with fur, trimmed with yellow cloth, and turned up at the toes. Some spoons rudely carved from reindeer horn, and several skins of the same animal, were also offered me and at prices that seemed reasonable. The children during my interview gazed at me with curious twinkling eyes, but the little baby, securely lashed in its leathern cradle, which was lined with warm felt, slept as soundly as any fond mother might desire. The cradle was suspended from a hook in the roof to keep the child from harm. The dogs appeared to share the beds with their owners. They were mostly ugly curs with sharp fox-like snouts, though two or three seemed a little better favored. When on the march the Lapps live in tents ; at other times they seem to prefer these turf-covered huts. Another of them which I visited, was only ten feet in diameter and five feet in height, but in this straitened compass there were living two families, numbering, all told, eleven persons. I could only look in ; there really was not sufficient room for the insertion of my body. No amount of wages will tempt the men to work. They pass the day in lolling around, smoking, and chatting. The women and boys, however, make moccasins, horn spoons, and prepare skins, upon the occasional sale of which they manage to supply their few and simple wants. One of the women showed me a Testament and a history of the Bible prophets in Lappish, but neither of these books seemed the worse for wear. A number of religious publications in the same uncouth tongue have lately been issued by the Norwegian government, but the Laplanders will probably never become bewitched bibliophiles.

I visited another encampment of the errant Lapps upon the sub-hills of the great mountain chain of Nordland, about fifty miles southeast of Bodo. The greater part of this distance was traversed in a small steamer, and the remainder on horseback and on foot. Having arrived in the designated locality, I took a Norwegian, speaking only passable English, as guide and interpreter, and set out at once to explore the adjacent mountains, for no one could tell me the whereabouts of the Lapps. All that we knew was that the smoke of their encamp-

ment had been seen a few days previously. I took
pains to provide myself with a pair of native boots
which, made of reindeer skin, were nearly water-tight.
They are easy for the feet, being stuffed with hay or
leaves, and are admirably adapted for travelling upon
the level, or up hill, but on descending grades, since
they have no heels, one is apt to slip. Having first
mounted a hill perhaps 1,500 feet in height and then
roamed a long distance over wild fells and moors, half
the time up to my knees in water, I gradually climb to
the snow mountains, leaving behind the birch trees and
reaching the zone of the white moss upon which the reindeer feed. Suddenly I fancy I see these animals upon
the side of a far-distant range of mountains. The guide
confirms my impressions, and we keep on until we at
last recognize distinctly a great herd of deer huddled
together in a narrow valley. There must have been
over a thousand of them, lying down in order to keep
more out of the piercing wind. They presented a
beautiful sight, with their dun-gray bodies, enlivened
by an occasional white one, and above, a perfect forest
of dark antlers. Near them we soon discovered some
Laplandish tents, on approaching which we were greeted
by a pack of about twenty dogs, who barked and snarled
around us, but did not commit any overt act in disap-
proval of our presence.

I entered a tent made of reindeer skins spread upon
birch boughs. It could not have been more than six
feet in diameter and four in height, but within it were
nine Lapps at dinner. Their ages and sexes, as ordi-

narily among those pigmies, one could not possibly
guess. Some were sitting upon their heels after the
manner of Oriental nations, others were squatting like
toads, so flexible are their legs. They were very
friendly, offering me some reindeer's milk, and also
begging me to drink some of their liquor, which was
passed around in a little silver ladle. Seeing however
the wry faces they made I was in no humor to accept
the latter courtesy. During the meal the dogs were
invited to partake of some milk and water from the
same vessel the Lapps were using.

Though their tent seemed so small, I may just mention that still smaller ones are employed in Iceland.
There you will find them only three feet high, five long,
and three broad ! The interior of the Lapponian portable pavilion presented a most curious sight. Its contents were marvelously miscellaneous. Besides the nine
human occupants there were crowded into it a dozen
dogs, an indiscriminate pile of skins, boxes, kettles and
provisions, and in the midst of all was a fire, with a
small copper pot containing hot water. Several large
chunks of reindeer meat were secured to the rafters and
upon a light frame of birch were about a dozen reindeer cheeses. The Lilliputians were representatives of
several families and were all men—at least so they told
me—save one, a woman who was their polyandrous
wife. . All were dressed in fur caps, woolen blouses,
leather trousers and boots. The woman in addition
wore silver ear-rings and several huge finger-rings. She
seemed a jolly good-natured person and upon my pre-

senting her with some gay-colored ribbons, was so over-
come with joy as to press my hand several times and to
slip from off one of her fingers a silver ring which she
with many kindly grimaces presented to me.   I willingly
accepted it as a souvenir.   Some tobacco which I gave
the men so delighted them, they said they would teach
me Lappish.   I was most happy to learn a little of it
and received the following brief glossary, together with
much laughter and many jokes at the expense of my
clumsy pronunciation of their jangling jargon   The
spelling is of course but an approximation to accuracy.
And I recognize throughout an intermixture of Norsk
roots.

| | |
|---|---|
| Father—Arahic. | Hot—Badka. |
| Mother—Adnic. | Cold—Choskish. |
| Daughter—Nita. | Brandy—Vidna. |
| Boy—Swinno. | 1.—Akta. |
| Good—Barrakit. | 2.—Koekte. |
| Bad—Shuka. | 3.—Kolm. |
| Day—Bavia. | 4.—Nelye. |
| Night—Edja. | 5.—Vita. |
| Fish—Quelli. | 6.—Kota. |
| Reindeer—Botsue. | 7.—Kyetya. |
| Dog—Birna. | 8 —Kaktse. |
| Knife—Nipi. | 9 —Aktse. |
| Fue—Tollo. | 10.—Lokke. |

Good-Day—Borris.
Good-Bye—Gor-nat.
Come in—Kap-mok.
How do you do?—Magto-veso?
Show me the way—Gunel-vega-deggo.

The fierce finkel which my new-found friends were continually imbibing from the little silver ladle (often replenished from sundry bottles), was beginning to make them a trifle too convivial, and so I thought it best to take my leave. But I could not do so until the hilarious hostess, with the ribbons about her neck, meeting me at the tent door, had again murmured her grateful gibberish and pressed my hands with some intensity. Alas! we may never meet again.

The language of the Laplanders is a Finnish dialect, with a great infusion of foreign and obsolete words. It has been said that these people were first termed Lapps on account of their small words and brief speech, though that is not the signification of the name Lapp itself. Their tongue is very peculiar in having eleven cases and three numbers but no gender. The general appearance of the men so strongly resembles that of the women that a difference of termination expressive of distinction of sex is not deemed necessary. It is said there are five words for snow and seven for a mountain, but that honesty, virtue, and conscience must be expressed by a paraphrase. Still, even if there were a nomenclature of all the good qualities inherent in human nature, it is extremely doubtful whether they themselves would ever possess or employ more than the mere names of such attributes.

The Lapps as a race are most lamentably ignorant. They possess no manuscripts and of course no printed books of their own. They are familiar, however, with many traditional histories and songs of ancient heroes,

which are mingled with the most fabulous accounts. I
could obtain, in English, only a single song as a sample
of their *belles-lettres*. The wolf, which forms its subject,
was once very plentiful in Lapland, but has experienced
so steady and unaccountable a decrease during this
century as now to be regarded as the most rare of
European Polar beasts of prey. This specimen of ver-
sification is as follows :

> " Accursed wolf ! far hence away !
> Make in these woods no longer stay :
> Flee hence ! and seek earth's utmost bounds,
> Or perish by the hunter's wounds !"

The Lappish mythology is simply a sort of universal
idolatry in which the elements are typified—a polytheism
by which every object in nature is changed into a god.
The Lapps are, I believe, the only race in Europe now
attached to heathenish beliefs. They worship several
Teutonic gods, and there also seem to be among them
remains of Druidical institutions. In not very ancient
times their rude wooden or stone idols stood within
inclosures of boughs where they were honored with a
variety of simple rites. At the present day they worship
five orders of divinities : super-celestial, celestial, atmos-
pheric, manes, and demons. Radien Athzie, the highest
god is believed to have created everything ; he was
assisted by Ruona Neid, the fruitful virgin ; and his
son Radien Kiedde kept the world in order. Another
god is Storyunkare, the lord of beasts, of the chase, and
of fishing. Tiermes brings sometimes weal and sometimes woe ; he carries the hammer; his bow is the rain-

bow, and in his wrath he slays men and beasts with lightning.  His symbol is a rude block of wood, which no female dare approach.

None of the Lapponian tribes have made any note-worthy progress in civilization during the centuries they have been known to the world.  The descriptions which the Greek geographers, Ptolemy and Strabo, give of the Phinnoi, and those which the Roman historian Tacitus presents of the Fenni, exactly correspond to the nomadic Laplanders of the present day.  Doubtless their many credulities formed a serious obstacle to evolution.  The men of the North, like the men of Athens, were "in all things too superstitious."  The very name of Lapp signifies a wizard.  Their witchcraft had even passed into a proverb long before the time of Milton, who somewhere alludes to "dancing with Lapland witches."  They had many signs which portended good or evil.  The stars, clouds, moon, the flight and appearance of birds in certain numbers in the heavens, were all regarded as omens.  They believed they could fore-tell the future, cure diseases, and exorcise evil spirits.  Their magicians prophesied by means of a drum, on which they painted the images of the gods and of things about which inquiry was made; having slept with this under his head, the magician on awaking told what he had seen in his dreams.

But the schoolmaster, armed with his primer, has been abroad in Lapland.  There too the missionary has been energetically plying his vicarious labors.  Many Lapps have joined the Lutheran church, though it hardly seems possible that these intellectual and moral, as well as physical, dwarfs should have the ability to comprehend the Christian scheme of salvation. Even when converted from paganism to Christianity, they are apt to retain all that is repulsive in their habits of life. At any rate, with the transmutation departs all that is picturesque and peculiar to them as a race. I acquiesce in the opinion of Taylor, that it is in vain for the romantic traveller to seek in them the materials for weird stories and wild adventures. They have become inordinately pious and commonplace. "Their conversion has destroyed what little of barbaric poetry there might have been in their composition, and, instead of chanting to the spirits of the winds, and clouds, and mountains, they have become furious ranters, who frequently claim to be possessed by the Holy Ghost. As human beings, the change, incomplete as it is, is nevertheless to their endless profit ; but as objects of interest to the traveler, it has been to their detriment. It would be far more picturesque to describe a sabaoth of Lapland witches than a prayer-meeting of shouting converts, yet no friend of his race could help rejoicing to see the latter substituted for the former. In proportion therefore, as the Lapps have become enlightened (like all other savage tribes), they have become less interesting"

In forming a general estimate of Lapponian character, a distinction between the dwellers in the highlands and those living upon or near the coasts, must be made. In the mountains they are haughty, suspicious

and morose ; while the Sea-Lapps are peaceable, hospitable, and light-hearted. The former are savage, the
latter domestic. But all are evidently disadvantage-
ously affected by the torpor induced by the winter
climate and their exposed mode of life. They have
no marked passions, save that for strong drink. This
is, indeed, their most noticeable characteristic. Anger,
theft, and bloodthirstiness, are all but unknown among
them. Even love is an almost meaningless word in
their language. They are avaricious, but, as a rule,
only that they may obtain money wherewith to supply
themselves with their favorite finkel. The manners
and habits of the gypsy Lapps have been finely described by the poet Thomson, who, in comparing them
with the martial hordes of the north, says :

> " Not such the sons of Lapland : wisely they
> Despise th' insensate barbarous trade of war :
> They ask no more than simple nature gives ;
> They love their mountains, and enjoy their storms.
> No false desires, no pride-created wants
> Disturb the peaceful current of their time ;
> And through the restless ever-tortured maze
> Of pleasure or ambition bid it rage.
> Their reindeer form their riches. These their tents,
> Their robes, their beds, and all their homely wealth
> Supply : their wholesome fare and cheerful cups."

The race of Lapps is dying out. Contact with the
worst products of civilization is effecting as alarming a
decimation among them as it has already made among
the islanders of the South Seas. The Maoris, or primi-

tive inhabitants of New Zealand, have decreased in seventeen years about 20 per cent. The natives of Hawaii are disappearing still more rapidly, as I have shown in a previous volume ("Through and Through the Tropics," p. 92). The census of 1878 registered 13,000 less than that of 1866. The reasons given for the decay of these two nations are love of drink, bad food and clothing, neglect of cleanliness, and unwholesome dwellings. In 1858, but twenty-three years ago, the population of Lapland was estimated at 30,000; while now it is given by an officer of the Norwegian government as only 17,000! The causes of the dwindling of the Laplanders may be briefly stated as, first, the practice of polyandry; second, the excessive use of alcoholic spirits; third, the failure and difficulty of obtaining sufficient reindeer-moss during winter, and consequent loss of their herds which supply them with food, clothing, etc.; and fourth, the being supplanted everywhere by the Quains, who are more hard-working and intelligent.

The usual fate of nomads, who are too feeble to oppose successfully the sweeping tide of civilization, will be that of the Lapps. They are inevitably doomed to early extinction. Without religion, without science or art, without a single high or noble attribute, living merely for the day, and not looking beyond it, they cannot long continue to block the way for more able workers in this "earthly bee-hive." From the south and east the line of civilization is gradually but surely progressing, and farther north or west they cannot go without emptying into the Polar Sea. Silently and swiftly they must disappear and vanish forever from among the peoples of the earth, leaving no mark behind them to show that they have been.

# CHAPTER XIV.

## THE REINDEER.

BEFORE leaving Hammerfest on my return from North Cape, I had requested, through a friend in Tromsoe, that the Lapps whom I had already visited on my northern journey should have a large herd of reindeer driven down from the neighboring mountains and gathered together in the valley for my inspection. Our steamer's anchor was therefore scarcely cast at Tromsoe before I was off, with an interpreter, up the barren Tromsdal, and toward the Lapp encampment. I had not gone more than half the distance, however, before what seemed to me to be a great herd of goats appeared upon the opposite side of the valley. I looked again more carefully and then perceived that my goats were purely supposititious.

We walked on a little further and met a Lapp who was lying stretched out upon the grass watching a herd of reindeer. My companion told him to have them immediately driven up to a corral, about two hundred feet square, close by the Lapp huts. So having hallooed to about a dozen dogs near the deer, the process of "driving in" was at once begun. I should explain that these dogs resemble the Arctic fox in everything but color. What the shepherd's dog is to the Scotch, the deer-hound is to the Lapp. The ingenuity and instinct, if not reason, displayed by them in collecting, keeping together, and driving a herd of reindeer are of extreme interest in their workings. Without them the Lapps could scarcely control their deer, for they become at times very restless and refractory. On this occasion these intelligent brutes would dash from the herd to collect a dozen stragglers and bringing them quickly in, would immediately dash out again and turn back others who were wandering in the wrong direction. They thus speedily massed the whole herd, and racing up and down the line kept them together and drove them forward at an even pace. The dogs yelped and ran as though it were rare sport for them, and the deer only seemed to move when the dogs were at their heels. At a certain cry from the herdsman, the dogs would bark much louder and fly about as if their very lives were at stake. It was an odd picture, the gentle and coy deer crowding together through fear, the yauping hounds, and the vociferating and gesticulating Lapp. On came the deer in a serried phalanx at a slow trot. The dogs seemed now to be working themselves into a perfect fury, but it was of no use, the deer would go no faster. At last I had them corralled.

There were eight hundred in the herd—low-built, delicately-formed creatures with huge branching antlers. Most of the animals were of a dark slate color, though a few were brown and some were quite white, with pinkish-tipped horns. They were hardly three feet in height and perhaps four or five feet in length. All bore antlers or horns ; those of the does being smaller than those of the bucks, while from the foreheads of the fawns only tiny spikes were peeping. Excepting those of a few very old bucks, the antlers of all were " in the velvet." Their great size contrasted strikingly with the comparatively small bodies of their owners. They were often as much as four feet in length, with branches, called brow-antlers, projecting far forward from their bases, and with spurs spreading out fan-wise at their upper ends. A Lapp lassoed a large plump buck and drew him from the herd that I might have a closer examination. At first he appeared quite afraid, making frantic efforts to escape, but the man holding him fast, he soon became so quiet as to allow me to pat him upon the neck. The reindeer are very gentle, except in the fall of the year and the winter, when they frequently turn and attack the occupants of the pulkhas. On such occasions the rider merely gets out and covers himself with the snow-sledge, against which the deer having entirely exhausted his rage, the Lapp simply turns it over again and proceeds on his journey as if nothing had happened.

I expressed a desire to taste some reindeer milk, and a woman started at once for the herd, while a man lassoed a doe for her. The milk I found tasted much like butter ; it was so excessively rich. The Laplanders either use the milk fresh or make it into cheese. The doe gives so little milk that a large herd would not afford more than what a few families could consume.

The reindeer cheese I did not like; it was too oily and too strong. A cake of it six inches in diameter and two inches thick sells for about forty cents. The venison which I generally ate at the hotels and on the steamers was apt to be tough and not very highly flavored, but when fresh killed and eaten on the mountains it is delicious. When the bucks are fat their flesh actually seems to melt in one's mouth. Reindeer meat is very cheap in the Norwegian towns.

When liberated, the great herd—herds generally do not number more than two or three hundred head— trotted joyfully up the steep hills towards greener grass and onward to the eternal snows. Their slatey bodies and white breasts and tails made quite a pleasing contrast with the verdure of the valley. The last I saw of them was as a swarm of ants upon the slopes of a far-distant mountain. Then I turned and walked slowly back to rejoin the steamer; my Norwegian guide, who had lived twenty years in Tromsoe, and who spoke the Lapp language quite well, giving me much entertaining information about the wonderful and valuable reindeer.

The wild deer (*Cervus tarandus*) are found not only in Northern Scandinavia, but also in Spitzbergen and Nova Zembla. Those in Norway generally live on islands uninhabited by man, swimming thither from the mainland. They are very shy and are shot only by being stalked, of course always from the leeward. The domesticated deer is smaller in size than his wild brother, and is a much less noble looking animal. A tame deer lives about fifteen years, a wild one sometimes twice as long. The reindeer cannot successfully be transferred to an uncongenial clime. Such attempts as have been made to introduce them into other countries have proved fruitless.

The reindeer are able to carry about 130 pounds, or they can draw over the glazed snow, when harnessed to a sledge, 250 pounds. In Siberia, a large species of this deer is ridden as well as used for draught. In Lapland one will readily travel ten miles an hour all day. It is recorded that a reindeer once drew an officer with important dispatches, in 1699, eight hundred miles in two days, or an average of sixteen and two-third miles an hour ! But this marvellous feat ended in the death of the deer, whose portrait is still preserved in the beautiful summer palace of Drottningholm, near Stockholm. An instance is also on record of twenty miles having been made in a single hour as a test of speed.

The wealth of the Laplanders is computed from the number of their herds. Two hundred deer are enough to support a family, but rich Lapps have sometimes as many as five thousand. Some of these people are very fond of money, and being exceedingly penurious (except in the one item of brandy), they soon accumulate what, for them, may be regarded as small fortunes. Thus the owner of the herd of deer, of which I have just been speaking, had besides it, nearly $5,000 in a bank in Tromsoe. The noble buck which had been lassoed for me was worth, its owner said, seven dollars. The reindeer, however, are a very precarious and troublesome property. In summer they have to be driven to the coast-mountains, in order that they may be cool and freer from vermin. In winter it is necessary to take them to the great interior plains where they may more easily be protected from beasts of prey. The reason that the Laplanders are comparatively stationary in summer is, that during that period the deer live upon grass and the leaves of trees, which sufficiently abound to render long transmigrations unnecessary. In winter, however, the Lapps are forced into vagrancy, because the reindeer on which they so generally depend, subsist then upon the sparse and widely scattered white lichen, and often have to make a long journey in order to obtain it. This lichen or moss is more abundant in Sweden than in Norway, and the colder temperature of that country is also found to be better adapted to the health of these animals. The moss flourishes only in elevated regions, and sometimes the deer have to remove as much as six feet of snow to get at it. This they do with their feet, and their forehead and nose, which are protected by a remarkably hard skin. When going on a journey the Lapps take a supply of this moss with them, about four pounds a day being sufficient for an animal.

The camel is not more necessary to the Arab of the desert than is the reindeer to the Lapp. But for this useful animal Lapland would scarcely be habitable. Its hoof is as remarkably adapted for travel in the snow and morasses of the frigid zone, as the hoof of the camel is for the sand and hillocks of the burning torrid belt. Hence the reindeer has been fancifully styled the Camel of the North. The wants of the simple race among whom he dwells are but few, and the reindeer supplies them with almost everything essential for the support of life. All that we derive from the horse, the ox, and the sheep, this wonderful little beast furnishes the Laplander. Much of the meat, in its fresh state, is cooked and used as food, but some, after being cut into thin slices, is dried or smoked, and then takes the place of bread, which would be a luxury to this people could they get it. They generally boil the flesh in the huge kettles with which every hut or tent is furnished. Standing around these, each person dips in his horn or wooden spoon and swallows the soup and meat while they are still scalding hot.

The pemmican which the Arctic explorers use is made from reindeer flesh. The idea was probably borrowed from the Lapps who, when they migrate from one part of the country to another, always take with them, for travelling provision, a quantity of the reindeer meat which has been dried in the air and probably also hardened with smoke. Pemmican consists simply of strips of venison dried by the sun or wind, then pounded into a paste and tightly pressed into cakes. In this form it will keep for a long time uninjured. The object is of course to compress the largest amount of nutriment into the smallest possible space. The lichen or moss (technically *Cladonis rangiferina*), so important a winter sustenance for the reindeer, is also capable of being used for human food. Its nutritive properties consist chiefly of the lichenin or starch which it contains. Its taste is

not considered unpleasant when it is boiled with reindeer milk.

In continuing my recapitulation of the services rendered the Lapps by the reindeer, I come to speak of its
milk, which they drink fresh, and besides make from it
a rank and unctuous cheese and a rich kind of butter
that tastes like suet. From the cheese an oil is made
which is the sovereign specific for frozen flesh. The
whey is used for drink, and in some instances is fer-
mented and distilled into an intoxicating spirit analogous to that called koumiss, which the Kalmucks make
from mare's or camel's milk. The skins of the deer
furnish the winter tents of the Laplanders, their blankets
and necessary articles of clothing, both for summer and
winter, and in short, serve almost every purpose to
which we apply cloth or leather. The antlers furnish
many requisites of their culinary and household apparatus. The women prepare from the tendons, by rolling
them with their hands upon their cheeks, a thread which
surpasses all others in strength and durability. The
only household gods which the Lapps have are also
made from the sinews of the deer. Finally, from the
sale of the milk, the cheese, the butter, the skins, the
venison, and the tongues—which are considered great
delicacies in the foreign countries to which they are exported by the Norwegians, Swedes and Finns—the Laplander can generally procure the means of satisfying all
his other wants.

This then, is a slight and imperfect view of the pastoral existence of a tribe of primitive heathen in the

Arctic regions of northwestern Europe. I desire only
to supplement it, in concluding this division of my
narrative, by a brief presentation of the rosy side of
Lapponian life "adapted"—as the playwrights say—
from the French of Buffon.

Neither the coldness of winter, nor the length of the
nights; neither the wildness of the forests, nor the vagrant disposition of the herd, interrupts the even tenor
of the Lapp's life. By night and day is he seen attending his favorite cattle, remaining unaffected in a season
which would be speedy death to those bred in milder
climates. He gives himself no uneasiness to house his
herds, or to provide a winter subsistence for them; he
is at the trouble neither of manuring his grounds, nor
of bringing in his harvest; he is not the hireling of
another's luxury; all his labors are to obviate the diffi-
culties of his own situation; and these he undergoes
with cheerfulness, as he is sure to enjoy the fruit of his
own industry.

If, therefore, we compare the Laplander with the
peasant of more southern regions, we shall have little
reason to pity the former's situation   The climate in
which he lives is terrible to us rather than to him; and
as for the rest, he is blessed with liberty, plenty, and
ease. The reindeer alone supplies him with all the
needs of life, and some of its conveniences; serving to
show how many advantages nature is capable of sup-
plying when necessity gives the call. The poor little
helpless native, originally driven perhaps by fear or
famine into those inhospitable climes, would seem, at

first view, to be the most wretched of mankind ; but it is far otherwise ; he looks round among the few wild animals his barren country can maintain, and singles out one from among them, of a sort which the rest of mankind have not thought worth taking from a state of nature ; this he cultivates and multiplies ; and from this alone derives every comfort that he greatly craves.

# CHAPTER XV.

## Over the Kiolen Fiellen.

In general I found the Norwegians exceedingly ignorant of their own country. Not being able to learn anything of value concerning my proposed route across the Scandinavian peninsula, I simply had to go on day by day, literally feeling my way and thus virtually exploring the country for myself. Nor do these people seem to have any more exact knowledge of time or interest in it than the Orientals. You might as well try to hasten the precession of the equinoxes as to hasten a Norwegian peasant. In making their plans an unpunctuality of half a day one way or the other appears to make no difference to them. I inquired of several of the residents of Bodo the hour of sailing of a little local steamer which ran up the Salten fiord, thus forwarding me about fifty miles upon my journey. But no two persons gave me the same hour. The average report would have made it at six o'clock, but it was ten before we were fairly off. The scenery of the fiord was rather tame, but there were some grand views of distant snow-capped peaks.

During the afternoon we came upon a sort of whirl-pool similar to the maelstrom of the Loffodens, only

much smaller. Our steamer not being able to pass until a lower tide, I embraced the opportunity to go on
shore to that part of the narrow channel where the
water seemed most violently agitated. Here stands a
small stone obelisk—smaller than that in Central Park
—erected by the patriotic countryfolk to King Oscar,
in commemoration of his visit in 1873. The miniature
maelstrom is in a huge basin which is filled and emptied
by the tide twice a day. The forcing of a great body
of water through a narrow channel causes the dangerous
current here, as is the case with the mammoth whirl-
pool of the Loffodens. The fishermen are accustomed
to pay but little attention to it, though occasionally
their boats are sucked into the swirling eddies. The
boats, however, are always cast up again after a few
moments a long distance from the spot where they
sunk. Men have been known to be ingulfed several
times, and coming to the surface have eventually been
saved. The current also frequently brings shoals of
small fish to the surface and hence, as I noticed, the
neighborhood was full of gulls. These alighted upon
the rocks by thousands, the flocks resembling falling
snow. So many fish are drawn through this channel
by each tide that quite a little fisherman's village has
sprung up there. On the shores of the inner fiord were
many fertile clearings around single-story farm-houses,
and also much grass land and many great fields of
potatoes. The hills were covered with scrubby birch.
At last we arrived at a little town called Rognan, at the
head of the fiord, after a ʻedious passage of fifty miles,

which we succeeded in accomplishing in twelve
hours !

Rognan presents a very singular appearance, since
it seems to consist of about fifty dwellings, looking like
boat-houses, placed in a semi-circle, with their gable
ends toward the fiord.   On landing I found that the
remainder of the village consisted of small block-
houses huddled together without any attempt at streets.
These being invariably closed, I had supposed the inhabitants were attending some fair, or had gone perhaps to a great hunt, or even to the town of Bodo.
But no, as there is a church at Rognan the people for
miles around come weekly thither to attend divine service, and these huts are used only as stables for their
horses during their brief visits.   The inhabitants thereabouts farm during the summer and fish at the Loffodens during the winter.   Not finding any decent lodg-
ing-place, I succeeded finally in obtaining a little cart
and horse with which to seek some farm-house farther
up the valley.   This I eventually accomplished, after
having driven through a pleasing agricultural district
and by the banks of a swiftly flowing river.   Though
the house was well furnished and had good beds, so in-
ferior is the Norwegian diet that I could get for supper
absolutely nothing but sour brown bread and some
cheese that would have put Methuselah, of Old Testament fame, to blush for his comparative adoles-
cence.

On the following day, having taken a long walk
over the neighboring country with a young Norwegian

who happened to speak fair English, we stopped at a
small farm-house to see whether its inmates could not
give us something for lunch. The house was a type of
many in the interior of Norway. It consisted chiefly
of one large sitting-room and a small dairy on the
ground-floor, above which was simply an attic used for
sleeping purposes. The walls and ceilings of the large
room were nothing more than the smoothed surfaces of
the logs of which the entire house was built. In one
corner was an immense open fireplace used for cooking the food and heating the room except in very cold,
windy weather, when, the draught being too great, a
coarse iron stove was employed. When not otherwise
occupied the hearthstone seems to be the favorite loung-
ing-place of the small children, who often stretch themselves out beside it at full length. A box bed stood in
one corner and a plain board table and chairs completed the furniture. The family consisted of father,
mother and four children. They wore dresses of
homely woolen stuff and the Lapp shoes already described. Five other of their children, they said, had
emigrated to America. The good people set before us
a huge wooden bowl of milk upon which the cream was
at least half an inch thick. This milk had stood but
twenty-four hours and yet the cream was so solid you
could hardly distinguish it from curd. The conventional method of eating it is with sugar, skimming off
only the surface. Consumed in this manner it is both
a wholesome and a luscious lollipop. Together with
some rye bread or barley meal it forms the chief and

choicest food of the farmers in this district, reminding
one of Dryden's line :

> " Curds and cream, the flower of country fare."

The only spoons furnished me were made of ox-horn,
and were at least three inches in diameter.  They seem
well adapted for skimming cream, though they are certainly several sizes too large for the average mouth.
These simple people treated me most generously, and
laughingly said that though their home and food were
not fine, yet I was most welcome to their hospitality, such
as it was.

On the way back to my own quarters, I met an
English sportsman hard at work with rod and reel, knee-
deep in a great mountain torrent.  Being without a letter
of introduction, I approached him in an apologetic
manner, not unlike that which Mr. Stanley assumed
upon meeting with the late Dr. Livingstone in Central
Africa.  "An English gentleman angling for salmon, I
presume ? "  "Yes," he replied, "I have just come out
for a little bit of fishing, you know ; my hut is over
yonder and if," seeing me travel-stained and tired, "if
you will be so good as to see my butler, he will give you
anything you want to eat or drink, and try and make
you comfortable while you wait for your post-horse—"
supposing that I was bound down the valley.  This was
indeed " richness," as Squeers would say.  It is needless
to add that I forthwith repaired to the polite fisherman's
"hut."  A short walk brought me to a brand-new cot-
tage, with comfortable sitting and dining rooms below.

and sleeping apartments above. The plain wooden walls of the sitting-room were covered with sporting miscellany. On one side was a small library, on another the gentleman's writing-desk. Opposite stood the work-table of his wife, who was also passionately addicted to sport. Consoles covered with London illustrated papers and a carpenter's bench completed the furnishing of the apartment. In the dining-room were imported china and glassware, and decanters of sherry and claret. From before the door the trees had been so felled as to give a splendid view of hill and stream, with rough snow-peaks beyond. When I add that the salmon in the adjoining rivers and lakes sometimes reach a weight of thirty pounds, and that this gentleman has his own English cook and butler with him, I have given you a fair idea of a sportsman's paradise in Norway.

I continued my journey in a clumsy cart upon the bank of the Salten River, which I had afterwards to cross to obtain lodging for the night. But upon walking to its edge I learned that the ferryboat was upon the opposite side and that all the people there had gone to bed. I mildly suggested the propriety of having a boat on each side in case of an emergency like the present, but the ferryman said that no boat would cross the river until the following morning, and thus was I igno-miniously silenced. By walking a mile down the river, however, I succeeded in finding an old skiff, in which I finally crossed and proceeded up the opposite side to a small village, where I was originally to have spent the night.

The guide much amused me by immediately striding into one of the houses—the doors of country-houses in Norway never being locked—waking the sleeping inmates, turning them out of the only room they possessed, and setting them at once to work preparing it for my occupation.   He then went just as unceremoniously into a neighboring house and brought out a partially-dressed woman, who saluted me quite cordially, considering the circumstances.   Nearly everything seemed to be cleared out of the large room, including a bundle of hay and a baby, and then I was politely asked to enter and make myself "at home."   The bed I found was of reindeer-skins below, and of sheep-skins above.   In one corner a huge clock, with a pendulum fully six feet in length, was ticking so much like a chime of cathedral bells that I immediately reached forth my hand and hushed its frenzied beatings—I trust forever.   Then, spread out upon the skins, with two tallow candles each nearly three feet in length on each side, I had a vague and dreamy sense of being laid out for a wake like that of Conn the Shaughraun.   In the morning upon arising from my crazy couch, so much wool and so many hairs from the robes were sticking to my dark clothes, that I had the appearance of having been tarred and feathered.

The utter ignorance of the great strong farm girls in properly setting the table for breakfast was amusing. Their custom is to eat from a common dish with huge horn spoons.   A plate for each person evidently would be regarded as an unnecessary extravagance.   They tried so hard to please me, however, that I told my Norwegian guide to thank them most heartily for the barley cakes, a huge stack of which was laid upon the table; for the milk, a gallon pan of which stood at my left hand; and most of all, I begged him to speak of my keen appreciation of the kind wish " Ever be happy" expressed in good Norsk upon the gilded coffee cup, seemingly a family gift taken from the mantel-piece. A hurried adieu—it is the same slightly changed word in so many languages—and I am off again across the river to the post-station. Here I found awaiting my arrival a horse fastened to what was but little more than a pair of wheels about a foot each in diameter. My trifling luggage was strapped behind somewhere, and a man, walking or trotting beside the cart, drove the horse.

The road was a mere track, full of holes, roots and stones, and led up and down such steep inclines that I preferred to walk most of the time. The country was not specially interesting. We were still following the rushing stream up the valley, passing several small villages and many fields of rye, barley and potatoes. There was also some good grass land. The valley could not have been more than a mile in width, and was walled in by rocky mountains, sparsely covered with small trees and birch scrub. Afterwards we wended our way through great pine woods. Much tar was once made here, but now the burning-furnaces are all overgrown with weeds. Soon we turned sharply to the east and entered one of the most savage and grand cañons I had seen anywhere in Norway. It is called Junkersdalen. Not more than two hundred yards in width at any point, it is perhaps a couple of English miles in length. There is but little more than sufficient room by the side of the Salten River for a road four feet in width—so that when two vehicles meet, one must perforce turn back. This seems a puerile ar. rangement until one remembers the fewness of farmers and carts, and the great expense to such poor people of building a road. Perpendicular and often overhanging cliffs of black rock line the cañon throughout its entire length. Their strata often lie at an angle of forty-five degrees. They are fractured and split and twisted and hung in such precarious positions as to excite one's alarm as well as wonder. The torrent thunders along in wild cataracts of foam, caused by the many huge fragments which have already been hurled from the vertical mountain walls. In summer, travel here is comparatively safe, but in the winter and spring avalanches of snow, ice, earth and rock are so frequent that the neighboring people dare not traverse the valley at all. Several of the peaks attain an altitude of 3,000 feet, and one of them, called Salvaagtind, a huge pyramidal mass of stone at the end of the pass, is over 5,000 feet in height. This stands a grim old sentinel at the portal of a beautiful valley of grass land where there are several houses, at one of which I succeeded in securing tolerable accommodation.

On the following morning I made what might be termed a seven-inch toilet, *i. e.*, one-half inch of water in a flat tin dish, one and a half inches of yellow soap, two inches of horn comb, and three inches of frameless looking-glass — total, seven inches. But why dwell upon such trivialities when I had the bracing mountain air and found awaiting me a restive Rosinante, clothed, certainly, though I was not so sure of his being in his right mind. It seems the kind people had improvised for me a saddle which consisted simply of a bag of hay, while the bridle was coarse twine. The former, with the addition of a pair of stirrups made of a couple of leather straps, proved very comfortable on starting out, but after riding a few miles I could have sworn there was not a spear of dried grass under me, every bit was in the ends of the bag. And so in unwonted imitation of the circus-riders, I was compelled to do a "great bare-back act" all the day long.

We followed the trail on and up the valley, fording the stream several times. It was one of the roughest tracks I have ever seen, part morass, part sharp rocks and tough roots. The horses floundered about and mine. fell with me several times, but I escaped with only a sprained wrist. In addition to this danger from below there was another from above : the birch and fir trees of the forest were so low and so thickly interlaced as to nearly unhorse us several times. Evading, however, the fortuitous fate of Absalom, son of David, we went on, constantly ascending, until we reached a region of moss and snow. Here we had not the slightest trail to direct us, my guide simply went up certain valleys and along particular ranges, in general directions which he seemed to guess at more than anything else. We mounted through the usual zones of vegetable growth—

firs, birches, and lichens. Several snow-clad peaks were
near at hand and I rode my horse across a few glaciers.
Crossing the boundary line, we lunched in Sweden and
from this spot gradually descended a long valley until,
late in the afternoon, the first Swedish house was
reached. As I feared, there was no food to be had there
save some sour black bread, old musty cheese, and thick
sour milk.

In the morning at an early hour I continued my
way, having engaged a man to carry my luggage. After
a rough walk of five miles down a valley, through morasses and birch woods, we reached a leaky skiff which
was drawn up among the rushes on the side of a small
river. In this we rowed to a long narrow lake, which
was traversed in half an hour, and then we had another
tramp to still another lake lined with graceful birch-
covered banks. The woods were full of young partrid-
ges, a number of which the guide's dog, a lively little
cocker, succeeded in killing. I had sent a man forward on foot to order me a boat here, and soon we saw
it coming over the lake, rowed by a woman and a man.
I did not object on this occasion to the woman's " putting in her oar," for she seemed thoroughly capable of
" paddling her own canoe." So on we went rapidly
down the lakes, for I had now reached one of the many
great chains of lakes and rivers which extend from the
sub-hills of Norway half across Sweden, and form the
water-roads of the neighboring farmers.

The farm-houses, which are invariably of logs and
painted red, seem mostly to be built after one pattern.

Down stairs there is a large kitchen, a dairy, and two small bedrooms heated by little stoves in the corners, and above them a loft in which the men sleep. You usually find about a dozen children in each, dirty and half-clothed, but apparently healthy and happy. All the houses have the huge chimney fire-places before mentioned. At night you can get neither lamp nor candle, an additional pine stick thrown upon the fire being the only method of illumination in vogue. There is no use for artificial light. The farmers do not read much and rising at dawn are so tired after the labors of the day that they go to bed at dusk. The knowledge of cooking is extremely limited, and the dishes served up to the hungry traveller are therefore plain and few. The culinary utensils being made of anything that will serve the purpose, are as heterogeneous as the paucity of their number will permit. They defy classification, each being unique. There are barns near these farm-houses which usually contain stalls for half a dozen cows and pens for the sheep and goats which most families possess.

I had a long "carry" around some rapids and then entered another boat which leaked so badly as to require one person to bail it continually. The boats employed by the farmers in this lake navigation are about twenty feet in length and four in width in the middle, with sharp ends rising high in the air. A small square sail, made of coarse bagging, is so arranged as to be hoisted and lowered by the steersman without his leaving his seat. When there is no wind the boats are propelled simply by rowing, which soon becomes tedious. The country can hardly be called settled, unless houses eight or ten miles apart would entitle it to be so designated. During the afternoon I re-passed the Arctic Circle. I had entered this remote region of the globe by salt water; I was leaving it by fresh. My circumpolar jaunt had covered more than twelve hundred miles of land and sea.

## CHAPTER XVI.

### AMONG THE HAPPY INNOCENTS.

AT midnight I reached Jaggvik, two houses and several barns situated at the head of a long lake called Hornafvan. The family had retired at the house where I called in search of some supper and a night's lodging, but they all—and there were seven of them—got up and cordially welcomed me. A great fire of blazing pine sticks was made and by its cheerful light I ate my humble meal of the omnipresent barley cakes and cream. I was given a bed in the kitchen, where four others slept upon the floor. My preparations for bed were curiously watched by the entire family. Several times after supper I was told (and as I had already made a fair acquaintance with Swedish, I understood) that there on the opposite side of the kitchen was my bed. I was only waiting until the young ladies should leave the room. Finally, seeing no hopes of their departure, I became desperate and boldly undressed and went to bed, saying to myself if they could stand it, I certainly could. The unsophisticated creatures nevertheless all stood their ground, chatting pleasantly together and laughing as if there could be nothing in the world so droll as seeing an American go to bed. Doubtless, with such surroundings, they were in the right.   Their kind hospitality, however, touched me deeply and I cordially forgave them their laugh at my expense.

At five o'clock in the morning I find prepared for me a very grand barge with a cloth sail, and three men, the father and two sons, to row when the wind fails. One of the young ladies also accompanies me.   I give her the place of honor at the stern and seat myself at her feet upon a pile of skins and rugs.   I tell her I am writing home of her lovely blue eyes and fair hair ; and bright answering blushes make her simple beauty a still more beautiful reward for my poor compliment.   She is quite happy and I am her friend for the remainder of the voyage.

The lake averages a mile in width.   The shores are very low and covered with birch scrub interspersed with firs.   At noon we stop at a small island for lunch.   This proves quite a picnic.   Upon landing I see put on shore a huge box which I suppose contains clothes or merchandise of some sort for a house near at hand.   But imagine my surprise when one of the boys unlocking it, discloses to view a luncheon sufficient for ten men.   There are dried fish, dried reindeer meat, dried goat's cheese, dried barley cakes and dried butter ; and yet, sad to relate, but far sadder to experience, with all this dreadful aridness there is nothing to drink, not even milk.   However, one who has been seven or eight hours in an open boat among the mountain lakes is not apt to be over dainty or exacting.   Anything edible that is reasonably nice then becomes toothsome to him. This Swedish bill-of-fare is only referred to here in order to assist the reader in forming an idea of the habits of the people. Their meals seem to employ at least a large, if not a very important, portion of their lives. After lunch we continue on our way, sailing when the capricious wind favors, and at other times rowing, until evening, when we reach the little town of Arjepluog, which stands at the foot of the Hornafvan. Here I find a very comfortable post-house and feel almost as if I had reached civilization again.

From Bodo, over the mountains and down to this place, I seem to have been witnessing a miniature history of culture. Thus from numerous characteristics of the bronze or barbarian age, my journey took me through the iron or semi-civilized epoch to the press or civilized age, and afterwards reached, at Pitea, the era of steam, and the outskirts of enlightenment. I began with the Lapps on the wild treeless *fields*, living in tents and travelling with their herds, which satisfy all their simple wants, both of food and clothing. Their domestic utensils were few and rude; their work tending the deer; their recreation drinking finkel. Next I reached the *fieldstue*, a rude mountain hut with scarcely any furniture and but one or two articles of diet, upon which all fed, thrusting their hands into a common dish. The cow was their best and apparently only friend. Though these people were Norwegians, they were so poor and so shiftless as to possess very few of the comforts or even conveniences of life. Then I met the farmers at the base of the mountains in Sweden. These dwelt in

houses with a spare room, which was heated by a stove.
They wore a little better clothing, though they appeared
to have no greater variety of food than the occupants
of the *fieldstue*.  But they maintained a flock of sheep,
housed their cattle in warm sheds, and had apparatus
for catching fish.  Their boats, however, were rudely
made of large planks and leaked continually.  Then
again, I stopped at a station where the people were quite
well dressed and had their hair combed.  Their barns
were larger, and some attempt was made to keep their
dwellings in order.  Afterwards I entered a house in
which the owner sat at the table reading a book, and
had his walls covered with Scripture texts.  He was
doubtless a very learned and pious man, but he lost my
respect by giving me some bad coffee and worse pan-
cakes.  Finally, to-day with the better-built boat just
described, and my present quarters, I seem to have
reached quite a high plane of intelligence.  Nothing is
wanting to complete my happiness save meat, white
bread, and ale.  But I shall have to continue my advance
in civilization still further in order to reach that sublime
development.

At Arjepluog, soon after my arrival, all the neighbors
came in to see me.  They so crowded about me as to
hamper my movements.  Waking or sleeping I could
get no peace.  Yet in general appearance I was little
different from themselves, not having the color or garb
of a Feejee Islander.  Had I possessed such a color, or
worn such a garb, there might have been some excuse
for their impertinences.  Never, since my travels in the

interior of China, have I been so much annoyed in this respect as in the rural districts of Sweden.

At the townlet of Afvavik I exchange the boat for the road. Now at last I leave behind me the snow-covered mountains. It is the first time for nearly a month of travel they have not been continually in sight in one direction or another. The change from land-scapes of rough rocky cliffs, snow and glaciers, to scenes smiling with smooth green hills and velvety meadows, is most pleasing. I go on toward the coast with a horse and cart. The horses are larger than those used in Norway and the carts—what shall I say of them? Simply that if the most brilliant constructive mind had ample time to consider the matter, I seriously doubt whether a more uncomfortable vehicle could be devised. It was merely a long box placed, without springs, upon an axle-tree, and at such an angle as to require all the strength of one hand to prevent one from either slipping out backwards or bolting forwards on the horse. It was filled with hay, and the only comfortable position I could find was upon my knees; but only fancy riding upon your knees for half a day! It is a revival of the tortures of the Inquisition. We progressed very slowly, for the jolting was excessively disagreeable, and I almost began to despair of getting to the next station when we met a farmer riding in the opposite direction. Him my postilion prevailed upon to turn about and take up myself and luggage. There were some springs in his vehicle, but the jolting and swinging were unbearable, and the rustic drove at a breakneck pace over a deeply-rutted road. We reached Avidjaur at midnight, in a half frozen condition. The weather was very much colder than I had found it in the same parallel in Norway.

There is a quaint old church at Avidjaur and a large number of the church-going people's stables. Riding through a long street of these, with every door and window closed, and recognizing neither a person nor a sound, makes upon one a peculiar impression. It is like traversing Pompeii. The distance travelled this day was about sixty English miles. I found a good large hotel, and after a short nap started on in a sort of two-wheeled gig, with very small and useless springs. The road wound through great forests of pine, fir and birch. Several farm-houses were generally found at the stations, and all the people, both men and women, were in the fields harvesting oats and barley, or mowing the grass. Some of the out-buildings, which are raised from the ground, are like the grain-cribs seen in our New England States, and this resemblance is increased by the long sweep-poles which are also employed here in drawing water from the wells. Swedish farmers have a very ingenious and admirable method of stacking their grain in small bundles about a pole, that it may be kept from the ground. A single roll forms a roof which protects the rest from the rain by the dexterous manner in which it is arranged.

The Swedish post-stations are large, with well furnished rooms, and a fairly good table. The sitting-room is heated, a few moments after your arrival, by huge piles of dry pine logs. In most of these houses you will find a few books. These are generally of a religious character, bibles, psalm-books, catechisms, and histories of the prophets. It is just the same among the farmers of Iceland. The pictures with which the walls are decorated are also of a religious character, and are usually executed in most glaring colors. These stations are much larger and more comfortable than those in Norway, though, as at the former, one is occasionally subjected to a great loss of time through having to wait for horses which may be far distant in the pastures. Another nuisance is this : during harvest time the men and women are accustomed to go far off into the fields early in the morning, whence they do not return until night. At this period you will find the whole village deserted, save for the presence of a few very old persons who would be useless in the field, and of a few houses occupied by children, who, for safety's sake, have been locked in by their parents. The children's safety, however, is somewhat equivocal, since many of them must be too young to take proper care of themselves. Then if possible you must secure the services of a child who can understand that you desire food and shelter and send it to find one of the field-workers, who will return and supply the needed hospitality. This is a matter perhaps of an hour, more likely of several.

The day before I reached the coast I had to wait two hours for a man, who then informed me there were no horses at that station. He assured me, how-

ever, that they would be found at the next post-house,
and so not wishing to be needlessly delayed by waiting
for horses that might never be forthcoming, I decided
to walk on to this station, a distance of about fourteen
miles, engaging a boy and a girl as porters. The road
led up hill all the way. We crossed by ferry a small
river flowing down to the gulf. The station seemed to
be upon the crest of the hills, for I had therefrom a
fine view of the fir forests and low hills upon one side,
and upon the other the Gulf of Bothnia and its hazy
shores a hundred miles away. As my ill-starred fate
would have it, they had no horses here, and also informed me I would find none at the next station, and
the following being the last one before Pitea is reached,
I began to make up my mind to pass a few days in
the health-giving but dull and dreary fir-woods. A
visit to the neighboring stables, however, filled me with
sudden hope, for there I found a teamster who was
going my way with a load of tar. Him I engage to
take me on in his old rickety wagon, the fore-wheels
of which are connected with the rear, at a distance
of about twenty feet, by two long timbers upon which
the tar barrels are accustomed to rest. Taking my
seat upon a central point between the timbers, we start,
but at such a labored pace that I have to take the
reins from my jolly wagoner, and thus we journey
onward down gently sloping hills to the coast. The
day had been sufficiently warm to burn my face and
neck terribly, but an hour after the sun went down the
temperature decreased so rapidly that I had to descend

from the tar truck several times and run swiftly to start the circulation of the blood. By midnight it had become so cold I thought that my nose and ears would surely get frozen, and this almost in midsummer.

At two o'clock in the morning I reach—Heaven be praised!—the town of Rocknas, situated upon the Pitea River, which here opens into a great estuary, across which I must sail in order to reach Pitea. The preceding day's work had been very fair—a walk of fourteen miles in the broiling sun and a ride of about sixty miles in springless carts, over a stony road. However, I found the station very comfortable, and, as usual, was the only guest. Rocknas is a long straggling town, lying in the midst of a great flat valley, with much cultivated ground thereabouts. In the fields the women were engaged in harvesting the barley-corn, using their hands and sickles in the same primitive fashion that was in vogue in the days of the biblical Ruth and Naomi.

Later in the morning I succeeded in getting a boat in which I sailed over the river and bay, in a couple of hours, to the town of Pitea. I passed several huge saw-mills, with planks piled up about them, and surrounded by acres upon acres of timber. Rough timber and sawn planks, together with tar, are very largely exported from Pitea. Sometimes as many as fifty vessels may be seen here engaged in loading these commercial products for transportation to foreign countries. Pitea is a very compactly built little town of about 2,000 inhabitants. The streets are narrow but

regular and in good condition.  The houses are almost
all made of logs and painted red ; they are usually one
and a half stories in height, with shingle roofs.  None
of the dwellings have doors upon the street, you must
seek an entrance in the rear.

I was much amused by the general style of the hotel
here, in the latitude of Iceland and consequently near
the Arctic Circle.  At the back, where the entrance is,
are summer-houses and tents, gravel walks and flowers.
The hotel is provided with a bar-room, a smoking-room
and several parlors, the latter being without carpets.
The dining-room is filled with small round tables.
Upon the sideboard is placed what is called the Smor-
gos-Brod, that is, the cold dishes with which both Norwegians and Swedes are accustomed to begin their meals,
adding thereto one or more small glasses of brandy.
Strangers are apt to mistake these gelid viands for the
entire repast, as the people eat so heartily of them,
and one sees nothing else upon the table.  They are
intended, however, for mere relishes, like the French
*hors d'œuvres*, and are believed to increase the appe-
tite, though, as a general rule, to eat seems a clever
way of destroying it.  There stood also upon the sideboard a large metallic urn, from the three faucets of
which you might draw Pomerans, Fahlu, or Renadt,
whichever you preferred.  They are similar, however,
being merely strong spirit with an aromatic flavor
which makes them analogous to the French liqueurs.
The Swedes, as well as the Norwegians, before sitting
down to a meal linger at this sideboard, help them-

selves to a wine-glass of spirit and eat voraciously of
each of the little dishes spread about. This Pitea inn
had a "Win Lista" which would compare favorably
with those of many hotels in the central cities of
Europe. But with almost all classes, as also among
the Norwegians, manners are much "below par." The
people rise from the table, run to the sideboard, take a
morsel with their fingers or anybody's fork, at random,
and return to their seats, eating as if shipwrecked at
sea. Napkins did not seem to have any particular
owner, being used by any and all until they were in a
frightful condition. Seldom had I such difficulty in
making myself understood as when, having received
one of last season's napkins, I endeavored to obtain a
clean one from the waiters. But perhaps I should not
be so censoriously critical in view of the fact that these
people are loyal subjects of one who is called King of
the Goths and Vandals.

Sitting in a chair and not on a three-legged stool, at
a leather-covered table and not a plank laid upon saw-
horses, I congratulate myself on the successful comple-
tion of my journey across the great Scandinavian peninsula with no worse result than a very sore mouth, produced by the daily task of masticating the adamantine
barley-biscuits of the peasantry. The terrible fore-
warnings to which I had been treated in Norway were
all dissipated, and I had arrived with a whole though
a sun-scorched skin. It was a journey of about 350
miles, performed by steamer, by cart, on horseback, on
foot, and in row and sail-boats. I had accomplished

it in ten days. My route led me across bays, over
mountains, along lakes, and down hills, to the coast. I
had seen the interior of Sweden and visited the peasants in their homes. My impressions of both are
already recorded, and I have only to add that this part
of Scandinavia cannot as yet be evidenced in support
of the correctness of the development theory. To per-
petrate an hibernicism, evolution here has not evoluted.
The peasants of the north are still lamentably lacking
in enterprise, industry, thrift, a proper education, and
an honest ambition.

The sights of Pitea were soon exhausted and I embraced the first opportunity offered of taking passage
in a little steamer bound to the south, and which
reached the town of Gefle about two days later.

# CHAPTER XVII.

## An Excursion to the Copper and Iron Mines.

THE most noteworthy mines of Sweden are those of
copper, in the province of Dalecarlia; and those of
iron, in the province of Uhland. The former are situated at Falun, a town about seventy-five miles due west
from Gefle; and the latter are near the main line of
rail which runs southerly to Upsala, about midway between that ancient town and Gefle, at Dannemora and
Soderby. The iron mines are a considerable source of
wealth to Sweden, though the supervision which the
government, through the college of mines, exercises
over this industry, is detrimental to its highest development. It seems that all mining operations are con-
ducted under licenses which specify the exact amount
of metal that may be manufactured. Heavy penalties
follow any infringement. This restriction is intended
to prevent a great destruction of the forests, since about
all the ore is smelted by charcoal. Nevertheless mining operations are making steady progress. The produce of the iron works is cast iron, bar iron and cent-
ner rails. Much of the steel is manufactured by the
Bessemer process. In fact, Sweden now annually
makes more of this steel than Great Britain. The Bes-

semer process is said to be as great an improvement on the older methods of making steel as steel itself is an improvement on iron.   In a recent experimental trial, a Bessemer steel rail lasted longer than twenty iron ones !

Gefle is pleasantly situated at the head of a bay of like name.   It is a pretty town of nearly 15,000 inhabitants, which rates it as the largest one north of Stockholm.   It does considerable business in ship-building, and in exporting timber, ore, and manufactured iron and steel.   The only two sights of which I could hear were a church and a jail.   From this I inferred that the good and bad elements in the population must be equally mingled.   Two express trains leave daily for Falun. At a station called Sandviken there is a large iron foundry where work of a most gigantic character is carried on.   A steam-hammer, weighing sixteen tons, descends upon an anvil of twenty-one tons, and forges iron plates of fifty-five tons in weight !   Steel guns fifty-one tons in weight have also been cast here.   The railway traverses a region of forests and lakes ; there does not seem to be much cultivated land.   In about four hours from the time of leaving Gefle, Falun is reached.   I could have known I was in a mining centre from the lack of vegetation about the town, the dirty appearance of the houses, and the copper roof of a church covered with verdigris, for I had seen the same effects produced in Colorado towns by the fumes of copper smelt-works. The longevity of the inhabitants, however, is said to be remarkable, and pestilential diseases are unknown in the annals of the province. Falun has only 6,000 inhabitants, most of whom are either government officials or miners. The school connected with the mines, containing an extensive technical library and a mineralogical and geological cabinet, is worthy of a visit.

The district in which Falun is situated goes by the name of the " great copper mountain." The mass of ore—copper pyrites and iron—lies in the form of an inverted cone. The rock formation round about is a reddish colored granite. These mines have a historical existence of a thousand years, and antiquarians believe they have been worked even as early as two thousand years ago. In order to inspect the mines and machinery, it is necessary to apply at the Mining Office, where a guide and torches are provided. One can also obtain there an overcoat and other suitable clothes for such work. The mountain is everywhere honeycombed by tunnels, drifts, and inclines. One sees a yawning crater with numerous galleries branching off to the workings in the interior. This enormous pit was produced about a century ago by the falling in of a mass in consequence of the unskilful manner of mining. Even now some of the excavations are in a dilapidated and dangerous condition. The external aperture is three hundred feet in depth. We descend by easily sloping, though slippery stairs, and find ourselves in a huge chamber, which must be at least one thousand feet square. From this open other and smaller rooms. In one of these a grand dinner is said to have once been given to Carl Johan (Bernadotte), his queen, and the Crown Prince Oscar.

On this occasion the mines were brilliantly illuminated. In several places I noticed carved in the rocks, and covered with glass cases, the names of royal visitors who had been my predecessors in the exploration of the mine.

A further descent of seven hundred feet is made by perpendicularly-hanging iron ladders. This is the lowest depth yet reached. The ventilation throughout is excellent. The machinery for pumping and for hoisting the ore, as well as that for smelting it at the surface, is admirable. Accidents to the mine or miners are nowadays of rare occurrence, but in times gone-by the careless mode of working often resulted fatally. A curious instance is that of a young man who was lost in 1670, and whose body was not recovered till forty-nine years afterwards. It was then identified by his former sweetheart, who had of course become an old woman. On being exposed to the air the body grew as hard as stone. In this state it was preserved under a glass case, but gradually fell to pieces, and had to be buried in 1740. In the time of their greatest prosperity, five hundred years ago, these mines were producing at the rate of five thousand tons of copper annually, but since the seventeenth century the yield has been gradually falling off, until now it does not exceed four hundred tons per annum. In fact, these once famous and prolific mines are rapidly becoming exhausted.

Dalecarlia chiefly consists of two great river basins, the population of which is about 175,000. These people retain more of their ancient simplicity of manners, dress, and mode of living, than those of any other part of Sweden. They also speak a language not understood in the adjacent provinces, which is said to resemble somewhat the Gaelic. These peculiarities doubtless arise from their isolated position, as well as from the fact of their thinking themselves a superior race to their more lowland neighbors in the south. It is from this district that the industrious peasants migrate in considerable numbers to Stockholm during the summer months. Their ingenuity is equal to their industry, for they are extensive manufacturers of basket-work, tools, clocks, and watches. In traversing this district of Sweden one falls in with many places memorable in the eventful life of the great liberator, Gustavus Vasa. Here is the cradle of civil and religious liberty, for here rose Engelbrecht with his brother miners and swept the oppressors out of the country; here the Stures found their chief support in struggling with the unionists; and here finally, after many wanderings, disguises and hair-breadth escapes, Gustavus began to carry out his great plan for the vindication of Swedish independence. Mementoes of this hero are scattered all over Dalecarlia.

Having retraced my track to Gefle, I next go by rail on a southeasterly tangent to the town of Dannemora. In passing a deep gulch, upon a trestle-bridge five hundred feet long, I distinctly hear the roar of the Elfkarley cataracts, which are second only in point of magnitude to those of Trollhattan, having with a breadth of two hundred and fifty, a fall of fifty feet.

Afterwards we cross the Dal River upon a stone bridge
with six great arches. Then we glide on through a
very beautiful country until we arrive at a "junction,"
whence a branch line, five miles in length, takes us
to the Dannemora iron mines. As I have said, these
are the most productive in Sweden, the ore yielding
often as much as seventy per cent. of iron. The metal
produced from this ore is largely used for the manufacture of steel, which is generally regarded as the best in
Europe. Singularly enough these mines are not situated in a mountainous or even a hilly district; but in a
marshy plain some thirty feet lower in level than the
neighboring lake of Dannemora, whose waters, in truth,
are only prevented from flooding the mines by huge
dams of hewn granite.

The best time of day to visit these, as indeed most
other mines, is at noon or whenever the charges are
likely to be fired. There are several mines clustered
together in this district. At Osterby, about a mile
from Dannemora, the ore is smelted and otherwise
prepared for exportation. The mine usually visited
is at Soderby. The entrance to it is, however, rather
dangerous. There is an excavation, perhaps five hundred feet square, and at least as deep, upon the brink
of whose precipitous walls are small platforms projecting far enough over to hold cranes which draw up and
down baskets containing the miners and the ore. The
ropes used are of steel wire and the necessary machinery is worked by horses. If you do not like this
method of descent, a succession of many vertical lad-

ders may be used. Arrived at the bottom, the guide
leads the way through several galleries to the scene of
the active excavations. The ore, which is obtained by
blasting, rarely yields less than forty per cent of iron,
and often the percentage reaches, as above remarked,
seventy out of the hundred.

The production of this the most important of minerals, would be much greater if more fuel were available. For the superiority of the Swedish iron does not
arise solely from the purity of the ore, but in consequence of its being smelted with charcoal. Notwithstanding the limitation of the government, the forests
in the neighborhood of the mines are nearly exhausted.
Sweden possesses some veins of coal, but it is of infe-
rior quality and occurs in quantities too small to pay
the expense of working. Some better coal is said, however, to have been recently discovered. There is considerable peat in the country and this of late is being
much used for smelting purposes.

Mining must nevertheless be considered as the most
important department of Swedish industry, for iron is
the leading commercial product of the country. The
working of the mines is making constant progress
through the introduction of new machinery. There
are reported to be nearly five hundred mines now open
in Sweden. Among them is the silver mine at Sala
and the zinc mine near Askersund. A mountain in
Swedish Lapland named Gellivara (Lat. 67.20 N.) about
2,000 feet in height, is said to be one perfect mass of
the richest iron ore, but its situation in an almost unin-

habitable country, far from the Gulf of Bothnia, renders it useless. This then' is a powerless rival of the immense bodies of almost solid ore found in Shepherd Mountain, Pilot Knob, and Iron Mountain, in our own "Iron State" of Missouri.

A few statistics in regard to Sweden's chief mineral industries, and I must continue my route south to Upsala and Stockholm. In 1877 there were raised nearly 375,000 tons of iron ore; 900 tons of copper; 50,000 tons of zinc ore; and one ton of silver ore. The pig iron produced in the same year amounted to 4,000 tons; the cast goods to 300 tons; the bar iron to 2,500 tons; and the steel to 750 tons.

# CHAPTER XVIII.

## Upsala and Linnæus.

Returning to Orbyhus, the junction station, I again take the rail southerly across a great plain with, at intervals, highly picturesque scenery, towards Upsala. I had decided, however, to stop a few hours at a little village called Old Upsala, about three miles north of the large town. This neighborhood is of the greatest antiquarian interest, both historically and topographically. There are three huge tumuli or barrows in which tradition avers that the Scandinavian divinities Odin, Thor and Frey lie buried. They correspond strikingly in appearance with giant graves I have seen upon the plains of Western Asia Minor. One of the Swedish mounds, supposed to date from the bronze age, is 64 feet in height and 232 feet in diameter. This certainly seems a huge knoll, but the work of the ancient Scandinavians could not compare with that of the Toltecs or Mound-builders of North America. Witness the great truncated pyramid at Cahokia, Illinois, which is 700 feet long, 500 wide, and 90 in height ! The mound at Old Upsala, whose dimensions I have just given, was cut through in 1874 to allow the Universal Ethnographical Congress, then assembled at

Upsala, to examine its interior.   Fragments of a skeleton and a few ornaments alone were found.   These I
afterwards saw in the national museum at Stockholm.
From the top of a neighboring barrow hundreds of
lesser dimensions can be seen for miles around.   Olaus
Rudbeck, the eminent Swedish physician and philosopher—who wrote a whimsical but learned work, locating
Paradise in Sweden, and assigning that country as the
common parent of the German, English, Danish, and
even Greek and Roman nations—relates that within the
circle of one mile from Old Upsala, he counted as many
as 12,370 of these singular tumuli.   Our own State of
Ohio furnishes a favorable comparison in this respect,
since it contains not less than 10,000 mounds similar to
those of Sweden.

A late writer tells us that "it was here, after the
dynasty and worship of Odin were firmly established in
the country, that the national temple was erected, and
the great sacrifices annually made.   Here, likewise,
justice was permanently administered by the kings, and
the *tings*, or great assemblies of the people were held.   A
sacred wood then surrounded the temple, and sacrifices
of every description were made to propitiate the deities
worshipped there, human blood being the most accepta-
ble to them.   On some occasions parents even immolated
their children.   An account exists of seventy-two bodies
of men and animals having been seen at the same time
suspended from the trees of this sacred wood.   The
temple was resplendent with gold, and the interior
decorated with the statues of Odin, Thor, and Frey

Even after the lapse of ten centuries, the name of Odin still lingers among the peasantry, though now only as a demon, and as such often used for that of the devil. Thus, ' go to Odin,' is in common use, and in some districts the country people still leave a bundle of hay for Odin's horses." The word Upsala signifies the "lofty halls," doubtless referring to this great pagan sanctuary. And a little granite church in the village is so old that it is conjectured that part of its walls may even have belonged to the still older temple. It certainly far antedates the Christian era.

Upsala was anciently the metropolis of Sweden, and is now its ecclesiastical capital, being the residence of the archbishop, the primate of the country. Formerly the kings of Sweden were crowned in its great cathedral. Thus Upsala is to Stockholm what Trondjhem is to Christiania. It is a pretty town of wooden houses, and contains about 14,000 inhabitants. Its attractions to the traveller are the Domkyrka; the University, with its library of 200,000 volumes; and the associations and neighboring house of the great botanist Linnæus. The cathedral is much grander and more magnificent than that in Trondjhem, which was completed twelve years before work on the Upsala church was begun. As with that, so with this: many restorations have taken place, often in quite a different order of architecture, and generally in the worst possible taste. It is in the austere Gothic style, built of brick, with stone portals. Its exterior length is 370 feet, its breadth 140, its height 105 feet. The nave and choir are supported by twenty-four columns. The chancel contains some fine specimens of stained glass. In separate side chapels are the tombs of Linnæus—a mural tablet of red porphyry, with a bronze medallion portrait; and of Gustavus Vasa and his two queens—three marble recumbent figures, flanked by obelisks at the corners.

The University of Upsala, founded about four hundred years ago, is the chief institution of the kind in Sweden. There are fifty professors in its faculty and it is attended by upwards of a thousand students. The latter are distinguished by their white caps banded with black and a small rosette of the Swedish national colors in front. I learn that no one in this country can enter either of the "three learned professions," (law, physic, or divinity) without having taken his degree at Upsala or at Lund, a city with a population of the same size as that of Upsala, situated in the extreme southern part of Sweden, and not over fifty miles distant from Copenhagen. A handsome building belonging to the university of Upsala is chiefly occupied by a library of 200,000 volumes and 8,000 manuscripts, some of the latter being very rare and valuable. Among them is a copy of the four gospels in the old Gothic language. It is named the Codex Argenteus, from the fact of its being written in letters of silver upon purple parchment. It contains 188 folios. It was made by Bishop Ulphilas over a thousand years before Gutenberg was born, and its preservation for so long a period seems little short of marvellous. Its highest value, however, consists in the fact that it is the oldest monument of the Teutonic

tongue. There are several other priceless literary treas-
ures in the collection. In proof of this, I might mention
the most complete copy in Europe of the Holy Book of
the Druses ; an old Icelandic Edda ; the Journal of
Linnæus (who was the professor of botany at this university) ; and the first book ever printed in Sweden,
*Dialogus Creaturarum moralizatus*, 1487.

An interesting excursion of one day may be made,
about six miles south of Upsala, to what are styled the
Mora Stones. This is the spot where in olden times
the kings were elected, and where they must mount
one of the stones to show themselves and receive the
homage of the people by *wapenbrak*, a mighty clashing
of swords and shields. Each king added to the circle
a smaller stone—one with his own name carved upon
it. There are ten of these rude unhewn stones still
standing. They are a little like those in England
known as Stonehenge, which name, by the way, is de-
rived from a Saxon word meaning hanging or uplifted
stones. Gustavus III. caused these interesting relics
to be enclosed by a stone building, on the ceiling of
which are inscribed the various elections of the early
kings.

Not far from the Mora Stones stands the unpre-
tending country-house of Hammarby, which was the
favorite residence of Linnæus—endearingly styled the
" Pliny of Sweden." Here he lectured to a numerous
auditory both of Swedes and foreigners ; and here
there is at the present day a sort of Linnæan museum,
with the apartments still preserved in the same style as

when occupied by the great naturalist, his doctor's hat
even, remaining on the table.   The lecture-room is still
here, but his invaluable collections were sold to England, to the great mortification of Gustavus III., who
vainly sent a frigate in pursuit of the vessel on which
they had been shipped.   It will doubtless be remembered that Linnæus, notwithstanding his acknowledged
reputation of being the foremost naturalist of his time,
was excessively vain, but the following illustrations of
that peculiar trait may possibly be new to the reader.

A lady of the province of Upsala wishing to make
his acquaintance, presented herself with a letter of introduction from one of his friends.   She was received
with much politeness, and the philosopher showed her
his museum.   Here she was very much astonished and
delighted at what she saw, exclaiming with a sigh, " I
no longer wonder that Linnæus is so well known over
the whole province of Upsala !"   Whereat Linnæus,
who, instead of the " province of Upsala," expected to
hear the " whole universe," was so angry that he would
show her no more of the museum, and sent her away
utterly confounded at the change in his humor.   This
great philosopher was besides so enamored of praise as
to be wholly incapable of distinguishing true commen-
dation from flattery and deception.   Another person,
knowing his weakness and caprice, once composed a
eulogy for him in the most florid Asiatic style, calling
him the sun of botanists, the Jupiter of the literati, the
secretary of nature, an ocean of science, a moving
mountain of erudition and other appellations to the

same effect. Though it would seem as if the weakest child might treat this as a farce, Linnæus, far from feeling displeasure at such bombastic and ridiculous compliments, is said to have interrupted the panegyrist at each phrase, embracing him and calling him his dearest friend.

In order to vary as much as possible my manner of travel I decided to go from Upsala to Stockholm by water, down the ever-winding arms of Lake Malar. Steamers leave every day at noon for the capital. Descending the little Fyris River, which seems to bisect the town of Upsala, we soon leave behind the massive outlines of the castle and cathedral, and enter a narrow fiord, with finely cultivated banks. Next we pass the chateau or palace of Skokloster, where live the lineal descendants of Tycho Brahe. It forms a quadrangle three stories in height, with graceful octagonal towers at each corner. Placed upon high ground and surrounded by beautiful gardens, its position and appearance are commanding and engaging. It was built over two hundred years ago by a celebrated Swedish general named Wrangel, and came into the Brahe family by marriage with that of Wrangel. On a signal from the steamer a boat puts off from the castle for such passengers as may wish to land. The temptation was great, but I could not afford the time for a visit. The interior of the chateau is kindly shown to travellers. It is packed with antiquities and curiosities, has an armory of great value, a fine gallery of paintings, and a library of 30,000 volumes and rare manuscripts.

We stopped, half an hour later, at the village of Sigtuna, which was, many centuries ago, the capital of Sweden.  To-day it has not 500 inhabitants, though seven hundred years ago it had 10,000.  In the year 1188 it was taken and destroyed by the East-Baltic Vikings, who among other spoils carried off a pair of church doors of pure silver, which it is said may yet be seen as a trophy in a church in the city of Novgorod I may add that in my subsequent wanderings through Russia and visit to that old cradle of its history, I took especial pains to find these " pure silver " doors, but without success.  It seems that the founding of Stock. holm, so much better a position for a metropolis, caused the ultimate ruin of Sigtuna.

As we steam down the narrow fiord we pass the royal palace of Rosenberg, a favorite summer residence of Charles XIII., and Bernadotte.  The scenery thereabouts partakes of a sylvan character, though we know from the large number of water-craft in sight that we are nearing a commercial centre.  The banks are becoming covered with stately palaces and charming country residences.  The fiord seems to grow even more winding ; its shores at least are more irregular. There are a great number of lovely islands.  On the right we pass the palace of Drottningholm, where the present king and royal family usually spend the summer.  The gardens, laid out in the French style, are filled with statuary, fountains, canals and pavilions. Here we have to thread a raised drawbridge which is part of the roadway leading from the city to the palace.

Half an hour later, or seven hours in all from Upsala, our voyage is completed and we are moored to the Riddarsholmen wharf of Stockholm, near the sedate-looking Houses of Parliament and a Gothic church spire which looms three hundred feet above.

# CHAPTER XIX.

THE capital of Sweden is one of the most picturesque cities in Europe. In so many respects does its
panorama resemble that of Venice that it has been
whimsically styled the Venice of the North. But in
Stockholm one misses the marble palaces and lofty
campaniles of Venice. Besides, the amount of their
respective populations differ considerably from one
another, for the metropolis of the Baltic has 35,000
more citizens than the " Queen of the Adriatic "—or
165,000 in all. If it be desirable to preserve the imi-
tative nomenclature of commonplace, I would myself
prefer likening this city to Constantinople, at least in
respect to its quaint and impressive position. However, retaining the old Italian city as the Venice of the
South, and accepting Stockholm as that of the North, it
would seem as though two of the cardinal points were
represented by these Venetian variations. Bangkok
with its semi-aquatic population, and its countless
canals and canoes, has long since been named the
" Venice of the East ; " and if one reflects for a moment, the Mexico of the Montezumas, where artificial
islands, reeking with floral perfumes, floated in broad

lagunes, might properly be accepted as having filled
the place of the Aztec Venice of the West. *Voila tout !*

Landing from the steamer and entering a droschky
I was speedily driven along the harbor, past the royal
palace, over a handsome granite bridge, in front of a
statue of Gustavus Adolphus, by a beautiful little
park, and at length was deposited at the Grand Hotel.
This I soon discovered to be one of the best hostelries
in Europe. The building is five stories in height and
has, I am told, three hundred bedrooms. It seems to
unite in itself the excellencies of the American and
English systems. Besides ample parlors, dining and
reading saloons, there are bath, barber, smoking and
billiard rooms, a **café**, telegraph and livery offices, a
steam-elevator, etc.

In the morning I sallied forth to see something of
the city. The name Stockholm is constituted of—stock,
a pile, and holm, an islet, from the fact of the city's
having been founded on a little island in the centre of
the outlet of Lake Malar, and of the piles having been
driven down across the channel to prevent the incursion
of the piratical Vikings. Six hundred years ago the
city was built upon three small islands, which still contain the royal palace and many of the finest public and
private buildings. Though the greater part of it now
lies upon the mainland, still as many as nine islands are
more or less covered with stores and dwellings. Communication between the various parts of the city is
maintained by means of bridges and little iron steam-
boats.

The streets of Stockholm, though often narrow and ill-paved, are for the most part laid out at right angles. There are a great number of small parks which are tastefully arranged and adorned with statues of Swedish heroes.  But few of the public or private buildings, however, are either imposing or beautiful.  The king's palace, an edifice somewhat in the Italian style, attracts more attention than any other building from its enormous size, its massive architecture, and its prominent position on the highest point of the central island.  It is built of brick faced with sandstone, in a quadrangle which is something over four hundred feet on a side. The royal family were not in town at the time of my visit, and hence I was so fortunate as to be shown over the entire palace.  This, however, was a rather expensive tour, for, instead of having one guide to direct me from entrance to egress, nearly every room or set of rooms had a different custodian, whose " itching palm" naught but silver could heal.  This palace, which was built about one hundred years ago, contains 516 rooms. The Throne Chamber is perhaps the handsomest of these, being richly decorated, and ornamented with choice sculptures and paintings.  It is 150 feet in length by 50 feet in width.  In immense stables near at hand are kept the state-coaches, and over a hundred horses, many of which are animals of extraordinary beauty.

The churches of Stockholm are not remarkable or attractive as a rule, but there is one, the Riddarsholm Kirke, near the king's palace, which deserves a visit from the fact of its being used as an imperial mausoleum.

It is the Westminster Abbey of Sweden. The distance is not far from the abode of the royal living to that of the royal dead. I find the entire floor of the church covered with the gravestones of illustrious personages. To the right of the altar lie the remains of the great Gustavus Adolphus, the heroic champion of the Lutherans. His sarcophagus is of green marble, and is environed with banners and trophies. It bears a Latin inscription which may be roughly translated as follows : " He braved dangers, loved piety, overcame his enemies, enlarged his dominions, exalted his nation, liberated the oppressed, and triumphed in death." In a chapel nearly opposite reposes the body of the fiery hero Charles XII., in a sarcophagus of white marble covered with a gilded lion's skin, on which are placed the crown, sceptre, and sword. In the sepulchral chapel of the present Swedish dynasty one notices especially a porphyry sarcophagus, copied from that of Agrippa at Rome, where rest the ashes of Charles XIV. (Bernadotte). On the walls of the choir are hung the shields of the deceased knights of the Royal Order of the Seraphim, the highest of Swedish decorations. Among them I noticed those of Napoleon Bonaparte and Napoleon III. The remainder of this church may best be described as a museum of war trophies—flags, standards, drums, and weapons of every kind. Service is performed here only once a year.

On a quay nearly opposite the royal palace stands the National Museum, which without doubt contains more of interest to the stranger than all the other public buildings of Stockholm combined. Architecturally it is a marble and granite edifice, three stories in height and of fine appearance. The façade is ornamented with statues and medallions in marble of such eminent Swedes as Linnæus, the botanist; Berzelius, the chemist; Tegner, the poet; and Wallin, the orientalist. On entering you first observe, and probably also admire, three colossal marble figures of Odin, Thor and Frey, the chief deities of the ancient Scandinavian mythology. The ground floor contains a magnificent collection of coins and medals; a mediocre one of Egyptian antiquities; and a very complete one of old Swedish stone, bronze and iron implements. The numismatic cabinet is one of the best in Europe. In some respects—for instance, in its Anglo-Saxon coins dug up in various parts of Sweden—it is even richer than the British Museum. There is a capital law in Sweden (similar to that in Norway) which compels a finder of any antiquity in the earth to present it to this museum, which at once pays its equivalent in cash. Among the national coins were some of copper which could hardly be designated as fractional currency with propriety, since one of them weighed forty-two pounds. It bore date 1644. Especially noticeable in this admirable collection are the large number of Cufic or old Arabian coins. These probably found their way to the Baltic from the province of Bagdad in the course of the overland trade which existed between the sixth and tenth centuries.

On the first floor of the building one finds many rooms of armor, pottery, bronzes, and engravings. The

second floor contains the gallery of Sovereigns, Historical Costumes, and the Regalia. This is in many respects similar to that at Copenhagen, which has been
precedently portrayed. It contains the coronation
robes and other dresses of the kings of Sweden from
the days of Gustavus Vasa down to those of the late
king. Here I saw the wig Charles XII. wore in dis-
guise when he rode from Turkey to Stralsund, and the
clothes that he wore in the trenches of Fredrickshald,
including the black felt hat showing the hole of the
bullet which ended his astonishing career. I also saw
the stuffed skin of the horse Gustavus Adolphus rode
at the battle of Lutzen, in 1632 ! The third and top-
most story of the museum is occupied by the picture
gallery, which contains carefully selected specimens of
the Italian, Spanish, French, Dutch, Flemish, German
and Swedish schools. Among the " old masters," I
noticed the illustrious names of Tintoretto, Cranach,
Vandyke, Rembrandt, Rubens, Velasquez, and Claude
Lorrain.

Out-of-doors, on the north side of this museum,
stands what is justly regarded as the finest piece of
sculpture in Sweden. It is by Molin, two nude youths,
heroic size, in bronze, and entitled " The Wrestlers ; "
though it would be more accurate to call it " The
Duellists," since it illustrates the duels of early times.
Upon the stone pedestal four exquisitely-carved bronze
panels, in low relief, tell a tragic tale. In the first, two
youths are seen sitting in a wine-shop, while a beautiful
maiden of whom they are rival lovers fills their drink-

ing-horns ; in the second, one has taken some liberties
with the girl which the other jealously resents; in the
third, they are shown stripped for the deadly duel ; and
upon the remaining side one sees the fatal result of the
quarrel—the death of one of them—and the girl pictured
kneeling and weeping before a Norsk tablet, upon which
the gladiators are engraved in miniature. The conception and execution of the whole sculpture are truly
admirable.

This form of duelling prevailed among the lower
classes of Scandinavia until within the last half century. Each of the combatants usually began by driving his knife into a piece of wood, and as much of the
blade as was not buried in it was then carefully bound
ronnd with strips of hide. So the stronger had the advantage of the other before the fight actually began.
The men were then placed together, face to face, a
girdle was buckled about their waists so that neither
could disunite himself from the other, their knives were
handed to them, and thus they fought to the bitter end.
Nearly always the combat ended in the death of one of
the combatants, and occasionally both were killed. This
mode of duelling was known as the " duel of the girdle." In the museum of northern antiquities at Christiania I saw the girdles and knives formerly used in
these dreadful feuds.

In Bayard Taylor's beautiful Norwegian pastoral of
" Lars " are some passages admirably descriptive of
this singular old custom, and which form, as it were,
a sort of climax to that poem.

" The two before her, face to face
  Stared at each other : Brita looked at them.
  All three were pale ; and she, with faintest voice,
  Remembering counsel of the tongues unkind,
  Could only breathe : ' I know not how to choose.'
  ' No need !' said Lars : ' I choose for you,' said Per.
  Then both drew off and threw aside their coats,
  Their broidered waistcoats, and the silken scarves
  About their necks ; but Per growled ' All !' and made
  His body bare to where the leathern belt
  Is clasped between the breast-bone and the hip.
  Lars did the same ; then, setting tight the belts,
  Both turned a little : the low daylight clad
  Their forms with awful fairness, beauty now
  Of Life, so warm and ripe and glorious, yet
  So near the beauty terrible of Death.
  All saw the mutual sign, and understood ;
  And two stepped forth, two men with grizzled hair
  And earnest faces, grasped the hooks of steel
  In either's belt, and drew them breast to breast,
  And in the belts made fast each other's hooks.
  An utter stillness on the purple fell
  While this was done : each ace was stern and strange,
  And Brita, powerless to turn her eyes,
  Heard herself cry, and started : ' Per, O Per !'

  When those two backward stepped, all saw the flash
  Of knives, the lift of arms, the instant clench
  Of hands that held and hands that strove to strike :
  All heard the sound of quick and hard drawn breath,
  And naught beside ; but sudden red appeared,
  Splashed on the white of shoulders and of arms.
  Then, thighs entwined, and all the body's force
  Called to the mixed resistance and assault,
  They reeled and swayed, let go the guarding clutch,
  And struck out madly. Per drew back, and aimed
  A deadly blow, but Lars embraced him close,
  Reached o'er his shoulder and from underneath
  Thrust upward, while upon his ribs the knife,
  Glancing, transfixed the arm. A gasp was heard :

The struggling limbs relaxed ; and both, still bound,
Together, fell upon the bloody floor.

Some forward sprang, and loosed, and lifted them
A little ; but the head of Per hung back,
With lips apart and dim blue eyes unshut,
And all the passion and the pain were gone
Forever."

In most of the large towns of Sweden there are
extensive libraries.  That of the old university town of
Upsala is the largest, and next in point of size comes
the Royal Library of Stockholm with 120,000 volumes
and 5,500 MSS.  These are contained in a handsome
and commodious building situated in one of the largest
parks of the city.  Among the many literary curiosities
shown me was a Latin manuscript of the gospels.  It
was known as the Codex Aureus from the fact of its
being written in gilt Gothic characters upon folio vel-
lum leaves, which were alternately of white and violet
colors.  From an inscription in old Anglo-Saxon this
work is believed to be about twelve hundred years old,
and to have belonged formerly to Canterbury Cathedral.  It was bought in Italy in the last century by
Gustavus III., who presented it to this library.  The
inscription is odd enough to be worth giving entire :

"In the name of our Lord Jesus Christ, I, Alfred,
Aldorman, and Werburg, my wife, obtained this book
from a war-troop with our pure treasure, which was
then of pure gold.  And this did we two for the love
of God and for our soul's behoof, and for that we
would not that this holy book should longer abide in

heathenesse; and now will we give it to Christ's church, God to praise, and glory, and worship, in thankful remembrance of his passion, and for the use of the holy brotherhood who, in Christ's church, do daily speak God's praise, and that they may every month read for Alfred and for Werburg, and for Ahldryd (their daughter), their souls to eternal health, as long as they have declared before God that baptism (holy rites) shall continue in this place. Even so I Alfred, Dux, and Werburg pray and beseech, in the name of God Almighty, and of all His saints, *that no man shall be so daring* as to sell or part with this holy book from Christ's Church, so long as baptism there may stand. (Signed) Alfred, Werburg, Ahldryd."

Here also I saw the famous Devil's Bible, so called from a hideous illumination prefixed to an appended incantation against robbers and maladies. This is a huge manuscript written on three hundred asses' hides, which were prepared in a peculiar manner. It was the work of Benedictine monks at Prague, and dates from the ninth century. From internal evidence it is believed to have been about five hundred years in preparation. It was found in Prague when that city was taken by the Swedes in the thirty years' war. The oldest book in the Royal Library, printed with movable types, is a *Cicero de Officiis*, from the press of Faust and Schœffer, in 1461.

In the southern suburb of Stockholm there is little worth seeing save the house in which Emanuel Swedenborg, the celebrated mathematician, philosopher, and theosophist lived. A small summer-house in its garden was his favorite retreat for study. Swedenborg has been dead more than a century, yet these mementoes of him are still standing and are religiously protected. The house is but a single story in height, very long and narrow, with small doors and huge double windows. The roof is covered with red tiles, through which protrudes in the centre a great dormer window.

The doctrines propounded by this remarkable man, and now enshrined in the church of the New Jerusalem, are accepted by a large number of societies in the United States ; though as a religious body the Swedenborgians have not had a very prosperous existence anywhere. Their largest American congregation is in Boston—that " hub " of isms. It is not necessary here to enter into any account of their belief, which is in fact only a phase of spiritualism unaccompanied by those vulgar and puerile characteristics which have brought the spiritualism of the medium into disrepute. But since Swedenborg was one of the greatest intellectual products of the Stockholm of the past, I will very briefly sketch the prominent features of his career. Born at Stockholm in 1688, after taking his degree at the university of Upsala, Swedenborg travelled over Holland, England, France and Germany. Upon returning he was appointed an assessor in the College of Mines. In 1721 he again travelled, chiefly for the purpose of examining mines. Then for twenty years he continued his studies with such ardor and success as entitled him to rank among the first philosophers of

Europe. In 1743, however, a new era in his life commenced, for it was in that year, he affirms, that he was
permitted to hold intercourse with the inhabitants of
the invisible world. He was then fifty-five years of
age. Four years later he resigned his office in the
mining college and spent the remainder of his life in
Sweden, Holland and England, devoting himself to the
composition and publication of his theological works.
That in which he endeavors to present his voluminous
experiences and doctrines is entitled the *Arcana Cœlestia*,
and first saw the light in London in eight goodly quar-
tos. All his books were printed in Latin, after the
fashion of the time, and were brought out in either
London or Amsterdam, since the press of that day was
not free in Sweden. His works received little attention
from his contemporaries. He died in London, in 1772.

The particulars of his remarkable transition, at the
mature age of fifty-five, from the rôle of scientist to
that of seer, and from philosophy to theosophy, are
given at some length in his diary. "Whatever of
worldly advantage," he says, "may be in these things
[literature and science], I hold them as matters of low
estimation, compared with the honor of that holy office
to which I have been called by the Lord himself, who
was graciously pleased to manifest himself to me, his
unworthy servant, in a personal appearance, in the year
1743 ; to open to me a sight of the spiritual world, and
to enable me to converse with spirits and angels ; and
this privilege has continued with me to this day. From
that time I began to print and publish various unknown

arcana, which have been either seen by me or revealed to me, concerning heaven and hell, the state of men after death, the true worship of God, the spiritual sense of the scriptures, and many other important truths tending to salvation and true wisdom."

Among the spirits who conversed with him in his visions, Swedenborg mentions, "apostles, departed popes, emperors, and kings, with the late reformers of the church, Luther, Calvin, and Melancthon, and with others from different countries." Some of his verdicts on past celebrities would be amusing, if they were not appalling. Thus he describes King David and St. Paul as among the lost; while Louis XIV., and George II. are distinguished angels. Not only did spirits who had once dwelt in this world in human flesh give him intelligence concerning the heaven, the hell, or the purgatory which they inhabited, but souls which never had been human thronged to him, so he said, from the moon and planets—with the exception of such planets as were not discovered until after he was dead. It is a pity he could not have told us about Uranus and Neptune—informed us less about heaven, and more about astronomy. He cleverly kept his spiritism well in hand, however, by being his own medium.

Stockholm is very liberally supplied with places of public recreation and amusement, such as parks, Tivolis or concert saloons, casinos, cafés-chantants, theatres and the opera. On summer evenings the concert-saloons are crowded and the music is generally excellent. At one of them I saw Johann Strauss, the

Viennese " Waltz King," directing the orchestra, his coat covered with decorations, and with the same old rhythmic movement of the arms and body for which he long ago became notorious. The opera-house is open during the winter five times a week, this of course, as in all the continental countries of Europe, including Sunday. The Swedes are passionately fond of music, and have reason to be proud of the two great singers they have given to the world—Jenny Lind and Christine Nilsson. At the Royal Dramatic Theatre, Shakespeare's plays and historical dramas are given. But it is of their Djurgarden or Deer Park that these people are especially proud, and with justice, since it is one of the most picturesque spots in Europe. It is so easy of access that you may reach it by one of the little steam gondolas in five minutes from the very centre of the city. The park is about twenty miles in circumference and is kept in excellent order. A portion of it is primeval forest like the Vienna " Prater " and the Berlin " Thiergarten ; " part is lake and stream ; here are cafés, music-halls, an open-air theatre or a circus ; and there is a lofty tower from which the finest possible view of Stockholm may be obtained.

I should not, perhaps, close this chapter without at least referring to a peculiar Swedish custom which is not unlike one I encountered in Japan. Many of the men's baths in Stockholm are attended by women, who scrub and shampoo one with astonishing nonchalance ; though not here, as I afterwards saw in Finland, does the shameless immodesty of the people permit the

sexes to bathe freely together in the public baths.
There, even families and members of several genera-
tions—grandfather, father, mother and children—take
unembarrassed turns in scrubbing each other's backs!
I will say nothing more than to repeat a former question—does not every country have its own peculiar
customs?—feeling certain that in this instance at least
the answer of the reader will be a fervid "Yea, verily."

# CHAPTER XX.

## The Gotha Canal.

To obtain a good idea of Sweden, one should certainly add to a visit to the capital a tour of the Gotha Canal and the intervening lakes. This great artificial watercourse originated in the desire of Sweden, in case of hostilities with Denmark, to have an outlet on the North Sea, since the latter country commanded the sole entrance to the Baltic. The scheme was first thought practicable in the early part of the seventeenth century. Swedenborg, among other noted men, was much interested in its progress. In 1800, a canal three miles in length was cut in the solid rock around the Trollhattan Falls on the Gotha River, near the proposed western exit of the canal. This was regarded as the most difficult part of the undertaking. In 1808, the famous English engineer, Thomas Telford, was consulted in regard to the best route for the remainder of the line. In 1819, a short canal from Lake Malar, not far from Stockholm, to the Baltic, was completed. Four years later long communications were opened between the Baltic and the great interior lakes Wettern and Wenern. Then the Trollhattan cut was widened; and finally the entire route between Stockholm and Gothenburg was

opened for traffic in 1855   The work had been chiefly
carried on by the army, which otherwise would have
been unemployed, and had cost something in the neighborhood of $10,000,000—much less than a " Brooklyn
Bridge ! "

The entire length of the canal, from Stockholm on
the Baltic to Gothenburg on the Kattegat, is 370 miles.
There are seven sections of canal, having altogether 74
locks   The length of the cuts is about 50 miles.   The
same distance is traversed along the coast of the Baltic,
and the remaining 270 miles are through lakes and
rivers, where the navigation is in many places very intricate.   The cuttings are 10 feet deep, 50 feet wide at the
bottom, and 90 on the surface.   The cuts of the Cale-
donian Canal, in Scotland, of which the Gotha Canal
often reminds the traveller, are 120 feet broad on the
surface, 50 at the bottom, and 17 feet in depth.   The
Scottish, however, has only about one-third as many
locks to pass as the Swedish Canal.

Though the original intention was to have a water-
way to use in time of war, it was found to be admirably
adapted for domestic and foreign trade, and for passengers wishing to escape the delay and expense of
passing around by the Sound.   It takes by this route
only sixty hours to go from Stockholm to Gothenburg
or *vice versa*.   The journey by rail, should the traveller
prefer to vary his route in coming or going, occupies
one day.   The steamers sail four times a week and run
night and day, which is something of a disadvantage to
the sight-seer ; though the most picturesque parts must

necessarily be passed by daylight, owing to the difficulty of the navigation. The steamers are small, accommodating only twenty first-class passengers, but they are comfortably furnished, and the table is good.

Leaving Stockholm, the steamer winds its way among the hundreds of beautiful islets with which Lake Malar is studded. Numerous villas are seen upon the banks, and the water is covered with boats and barges of all sizes and shapes. The first town at which we stop is that of Sodertelge, about twenty miles from the capital, whose inhabitants frequent it as a bathing-place. Here is the first cutting. It extends about two miles through sandy ravines and has but one lock. We pass several fine old castles upon each shore, and threading our way among innumerable islands, finally emerge into the sea. Two hours later we are steaming up a beautiful fiord to the town of Soderkoping, whence the canal proceeds through several locks, between two mountains, and out into a little lake, and then again becomes a canal, until we reach Lake Roxen, a pretty and pellucid expanse about fifteen miles in length and six in width. Beyond this body of water there are sixteen locks which, with those already passed, raise the canal 245 feet above the Baltic. Another small lake being passed over, we arrive at the town of Motala, where are situated the largest iron foundries and steam-engine manufactories in Sweden. Here are also paper mills and match factories. Not far distant from Motala is the grave of Baron von Platen, a Swedish engineer, who might properly be called the founder of the canal as it now exists.

Lake Wettern, a body of water eighty miles in length, and narrow, but very deep, is crossed in less than an hour, and soon after Lake Viken, 398 feet above sea-level and the highest point on the canal, is reached. From here, the steamer slowly descends through long cuttings and basins, until we reach Lake Wenern, where the scenery is very beautiful so long as we remain in sight of land. This is the largest lake in Sweden, and the third in Europe in regard to its dimensions, the first and second being Lakes Ladoga and Onega in Russia. It is about a hundred miles in length, by fifty in width, and in many places is said to be upwards of 300 feet in depth. The water of these great inland lakes is like that of a clear spring. At the southern extremity of Lake Wenern is the town of Wernersberg, where we land some cargo, and then rush on down the Gotha River to Trollhattan. Here are the famous falls which necessitated the most stupendous rock cutting of the entire canal, and to which I have already referred. The difference in level from the point at which this cutting leaves the river, above the falls, to the point where it joins it again, is 120 feet. In passing, nine locks are employed, and since this requires about two hours, the passenger has ample time to inspect the falls.

The word Trollhattan signifies the "home of the water-witches," and when one sees the bright foaming water rushing past the dark fir-covered islands and dashing upon the rocks below, with a roar which renders conversation impossible, the poetry of the Swedish name seems not misapplied. But in truth, these leaping torrents are rather cataracts than falls. They number seven, the highest being but 44 feet, and all combined having an altitude of only 112 feet. The lack of greater height (which one fresh from the fosses of Norway is apt to expect) is amply compensated for by the vast volume of water which is always in the river, and which is so much missed in the Norwegian falls, at least during the summer months. On our way down alongside these cataracts, the guide shows us what is called the Kungsgrottan or King's Cave, a curious excavation in the solid rock, upon which are carved the names of many Swedish kings who have visited the home of the water-witches. This custom is similar to that of the Assyrian and Moabite monarchs, who were in the habit of recording their victories in inscriptions on the rocks. The Trollhattan rock is especially interesting when considered from a geological standpoint. It is in the form of a smoothly-polished hemisphere, and must, at some very remote period, have formed a portion of the bed of a glacier whose torrents, whirling around loose stones, gradually carved its surface and drilled holes in it like the "giant's caldrons" or pot-holes found in England and in Switzerland.

Within three or four hours after rejoining the course of the river, we are at Gothenburg, having passed through a beautiful region dotted with farm-houses, churches, and manufactories. This, the western terminus of the great canal, is the second city and first commercial port of Sweden. Its present population is about 70,000. It is connected by railway with all the principal cities of Sweden and Norway. It daily communicates by steamer with Denmark ; and in like fashion it communicates weekly with Hamburg, Amsterdam, London, Havre, and New York. The town is built on the Dutch plan, reminding one of Rotterdam with its intersecting canals covered with picturesque craft. The streets of Gothenburg are well paved and the houses, mostly of brick and three stories in height, have a plain but comfortable appearance. In the principal square stands a large bronze statue of the founder of the city, Gustavus Adolphus. The exports from Gothenburg are those of Sweden in general—bar-iron, timber, and corn ; and so likewise are the imports— textile manufactures, coals and colonial produce. I might add that the total exports of Sweden in 1878 amounted, in round numbers, to $63,000,000 and the imports in the same year, to $80,000,000.

Two express trains leave Gothenburg daily for Stockholm, passing between the great lakes Wenern and Wettern, and connecting midway on their route with the railroad from Christiania. The railway-carriages are similar to those used in Germany. The line passes through a richly-wooded and often highly-cultivated and undulating country, diversified by dark hills, sparkling waterfalls, gray ruins, and quaint villages. Occasionally I see the picturesque national costumes of the peasants. No town upon the road, however, is of sufficient importance or interest to detain me. Leaving Gothenburg early in the morning, I arrive at the capital in the evening.

A brief comparison of the sister countries to which this volume is mainly devoted, will at least prove instructive, if not very entertaining. Sweden is remarkably like Norway in its dimensions. Thus, its greatest length is only one hundred miles less than that of Norway, and its greatest width only twenty-five miles less. But so narrow is the greater part of Norway that the area of Sweden exceeds it by about 50,000 square miles. Sweden differs very much from Norway in the fact that it is for the most part a level country filled with rivers and lakes. There is a community of structure, however, in the forests of pine, fir and birch which cover about half the surface of each country. Norway contains several mines, but they are not, like those of Sweden, remarkable for their copper, zinc and iron.

Sweden possesses more than double the population of Norway ; though again there is a similarity in that about three-fourths of the inhabitants of each country are devoted to agricultural pursuits. Among both nations a person can rarely be met who can neither read nor write. As in Norway, so in some of those parts of Sweden which are very thinly settled, the schools are moved from point to point so as to reach all the people. Instruction is here gratuitous and compulsory, and those children not attending schools under the supervision of the government must furnish proofs of having been privately educated. In 1877, 98 per cent. of all the children between eight and fifteen years of age attended the public schools. In France

75 per cent of those between five and fifteen attend school; in England 72, and in the United States 82 per cent. The high schools of the towns of Sweden are capitally managed. As previously mentioned, the University of Upsala, with over 1,000 students, has an enviable celebrity. It is calculated that of the total male population of the kingdom one in every 668 enjoys a liberal or university education. The government has lately introduced the Metric System into both Sweden and Norway. One hundred and fifty newspapers are said to exist in Sweden, very many more than are published in Norway. The Swedes have singular, though just, laws concerning the public press. Although the press is free, editors are held responsible for what they publish. If accused of false statement they are immediately tried. The prosecutor, the accused, and the court together choose a jury of nine persons, and a two-thirds vote of these is decisive.

Sweden much surpasses Norway in the number of its railways and steamers. In Sweden, 3,500 miles are now opened; while more than 200 steamers are engaged in coast and inland navigation. The railways are built partly at the cost of the State. In 1879, the Diet voted nearly $2,500,000 for the construction of new railroads. Telegraph lines cover both Norway and Sweden, the charge being about thirty cents for twenty words sent anywhere in the peninsula. The total length of the telegraph wires in Sweden is nearly 18,000 miles.

Emigration from both Norway and Sweden (mostly to the United States) commenced in recent years, and showed at first signs of increasing, but is now on the wane. In 1869, there were 39,064 Swedish emigrants ; five years later, the annual rate had fallen to 7,791 ; and in 1876, it had only risen again to 9,418.

Most European countries at the present day possess colonies in some part or other of the world, and Sweden barely escapes being an exception, for her single colony is the diminutive island of St. Bartholomew, in the West Indies. A hundred years ago this island was ceded by France to Sweden. It has an area of about thirty square miles, and ten thousand inhabitants. Two-thirds of these are negroes who were formerly slaves, but were emancipated by the Swedish government in 1847. This little Caribbean island is hilly in the interior and quite fertile, but though cotton, sugar, and indigo are produced, only cattle and salt are exported.

# CHAPTER XXI.

## The Grand Duchy of Finland.

Twice a week a capacious iron steamer leaves Stockholm for St. Petersburg, touching at four of the chief towns of Finland. The time required to traverse this route is four days. Though the coast scenery is said to be far more interesting than that inland, I thought it would be better to break my voyage at the second stopping-place of the steamer, namely Helsingfors, the modern capital of Finland, and thence journey overland by rail through the most thickly settled districts of the country, to the town of Wiborg, and then on to St. Petersburg. This would give me an opportunity to see something more of the peasants and the agricultural condition of the interior.

For some time after leaving Stockholm we threaded our way among the many rocky islets which skirt the Swedish coast. Then we had about six hours of the " open sea " of the Gulf of Bothnia, which as usual, owing to its shallowness, afforded us a placid sail. In winter, a few miles north of our course, there is a road over the ice from Sweden to Finland, and here in 1809 Barclay de Tolly crossed with a division of the Russian army. The post is now regularly carried by this route upon the closing of navigation. But here we are again slowly feeling our way through a similar fringe of islets to those we had only recently left on the opposite side of the gulf.

The first view of Abo is rather fine, with its old castle on a hill and its houses painted red. The city is built beside a little river, in which the steamer casts anchor. The passports being examined and the luggage searched by the customs officials, we are at liberty to land. Near at hand on the quay I find a large and good hotel called the Societats-hus. Abo is the most ancient city in Finland, having been founded more than seven hundred years ago. At first one is struck by its straggling appearance, knowing that it contains nearly 23,000 inhabitants. This peculiarity is soon explained, however, by the width of the streets, the lowness of the houses, and the number of seemingly eligible sites unoccupied. The city was once dreadfully ravaged by fire, and when it was rebuilt the houses were purposely thus placed far apart. What with fires, the removal of its university and library to Helsingfors, and its diminishing trade, the glory of Abo has well-nigh departed.

The remote era of the founding of this city recalls the early history of Finland, which I find, as is usual in all that relates to native story, full of obscurity. In fact nothing is certainly known of this wild and cold country before the twelfth century. In 1157 a king of Sweden named Eric, at the instigation of the Pope, undertook a crusade against the Finns, with the unequally laudable objects of converting them, and of punishing them for their depredations on the Swedish coast.   A century later, the power of Sweden was firmly established in Finland, and remained dominant for nearly four hundred years.   In 1699, however, began a war with Russia, which continued with varying fortunes until 1721.   In that year a peace was signed which ceded to Russia the province of Wiborg, that adjoining Lake Ladoga.   At about this period, it is said, the population of Finland amounted to 250,000. It has now reached a total of 1,800,000, ·exactly the same number that Norway contains, and about 200,000 less than that of Denmark.   Before many years the Swedes, anxious to gain possession of their lost provinces, declared war again.   But their army was in such a disorganized state that only defeat could follow.   Besides, there were political factions at home, and conspiracies among the troops abroad.   But notwithstanding all these discouragements and hindrances, a naval victory of the Swedes, in 1790, finally resulted in a peace with Russia by which all matters were suffered to remain on the basis on which they had stood before the war.   Still another conflict, happily the last, ended in the conquest of Finland by the Russians, and the assurance to the Finns by the Emperor Alexander I. that their religion and the integrity of their constitutions were to be maintained and protected.

The steamer, following the coast to the eastward, reaches Helsingfors in about twelve hours after leaving Abo.   This, the capital of the country and the seat of the Senate, has a population of nearly 35,000.   It was founded by Gustavus Vasa of Sweden, in the sixteenth century. The approach to Helsingfors from the Gulf of Finland is very striking. The harbor is protected by the fortress of Sweaborg, built on seven islands and regarded as so impregnable as to receive the title of the Gibraltar of the North. Helsingfors has the appearance of a Russian rather than of a Swedish town. The streets are broad and arranged at right angles ; the houses are large and regular. The harbor front is lined with a handsome granite quay. Some of the public buildings are worth visiting. My Finn guide certainly took great pride in showing me the museum of the university, containing a rich collection of the zoology of the country ; the cathedral of the Assumption, from the dome of which a fine view is obtained ; and the theatre, built after the model of the Dresden Opera-house, where performances during the season are given, in the Swedish language, four times a week. Afterwards I was convoyed about the Botanical Garden, whence splendid views of the surrounding country are to be obtained.

In the Senate House, the late Emperor Alexander II. has several times presided in person, and you are shown a splendid throne upon which he sat in state. Finland, the reader is aware, is a Grand Duchy of that empire which comprises one-seventh of the territorial part of the globe. Like Poland it is ruled by a Governor-General, assisted by the Imperial Senate, over which a representative of the Emperor regularly presides. Then at St. Petersburg dwells a sort of Secretary of

State for Finland, whose offices are similar to those of the British Secretary of State for India. So it will be seen that this Grand Duchy is in a manner independent. It pays no tribute to Russia, and the consent of the Diet must be obtained for the introduction of new laws and new taxes.

The University of Helsingfors has four faculties, forty professors, and nearly seven hundred students. The remains of the library, which were saved from the great fire at Abo, are preserved in the Ritter Haus or Hall of Nobles, and consist of about 150,000 volumes. Printing was introduced into Finland in 1641. This library then contained only twenty-one books and a globe.

Professor Nordenskiöld, the famous explorer of the northern seas, who is a Finn by birth, though now a Swedish subject, was educated at the university here in 1849–53. He passed "first" in all the examinations, and was afterwards appointed Director of the Faculty of Mathematics and Physics. But his taste was rather toward natural history, in the highest branches of which he labored incessantly. He had already written some works on mineralogy, which are still regarded as valuable. In 1856, Professor Nordenskiöld was offered his choice between the chair of Mineralogy and Geology, or an appointment to proceed on a voyage of exploration. He chose the latter but hesitated so long that another appointment was made in his stead. About this time he received from his Alma Mater, the University of Helsingfors, his degrees of Master of Arts and Doctor of Philosophy. The cause of his leaving Finland and obtain-

ing letters of naturalization as a Swedish subject, was his
persecution by the authorities on account of his frequent
interference in the politics of the Grand Duchy, with
which he never was in accord. In changing his country,
however, he did not change his political views either in
theory or practice, for he sat and voted in the Chamber
of Nobles during the last two Assemblies of the Swedish
States, and for several years was Liberal member for
Stockholm.

In 1876, it will be remembered, Nordenskiöld visited
the United States, and was honored by the American
Geographical Society with an invitation to a public re-
ception, in the city of New York, at which other specially
invited guests were to be present, namely, H. M. the
Emperor of Brazil, the late Dr. Aug. Peterman the eminent cartographer, and Dr. C. H. Berendt, the highest
living authority upon the ancient civilizations of Central
America. Unfortunately, however, for the members of
the Society, Professor Nordenskiöld was not able to
accept the invitation, as he was compelled to leave for
Europe two days before the meeting, that he might be
in time for the starting of a new expedition to the Arctic,
planned and headed by himself. This expedition, which,
like that of the previous year, had for its object the
exploration of the great Siberian rivers, was in the end
satisfactorily accomplished. For no less worthy a purpose, or successful a performance, would the members
of the A. G. S. have foregone so sudden a departure of
a scholar and discoverer entitled to supereminent respect and praise.

The last exploration of Nordenskiöld, as all my readers know, forms a most brilliant part of the great history of Arctic navigation.   Leaving Tromsoe, on the west coast of Norway, in the midsummer of 1878, with the avowed intention of not only reaching the mouth of the Lena River in Siberia, but of actually pushing on further to the east until an exit might be gained from the Arctic to the Pacific Ocean, *via* Behring's Straits, he was unfortunately embayed in the ice at a point only a few hundred miles to the westward of his objective point.   Here he was compelled to remain until the following summer, when the anxious world again heard of him at Japan.   The "northeast passage," had at last been discovered, 326 years after the first expedition of which we know, that of Willoughby and Chancellor, and twenty-seven years after the " northwest passage," around America, was proved to exist by M'Clure.  Nordenskiöld's triumphal journey to Stockholm—thus completing for the first time in the annals of the world, the circumnavigation of Asia and Europe—is matter of too recent occurrence to demand more than a passing notice in these pages.

It is said that the total expenses of this most successful expedition amount to about $125,000, considerably less than half the cost of Captain Nares' recent Polar exploration, which resulted in almost complete failure.   Of the first mentioned sum the King of Sweden, the Russian banker, M. Sibirikoff, and Mr. Dickson, the Gothenburg merchant, each contributed about $35,000.   The remainder was paid by the Swedish exchequer.   Professor Nordenskiöld has nearly finished writing his history of "The Voyage of the Vega," which will be published simultaneously in Sweden, Russia, Germany, Italy, France, England, and America. I know of but one other narrative of exploration which has ever in the history of literature received more varied linguistic and national honors at its birth, and that is Stanley's "Through the Dark Continent," which he informed me—in the summer of 1878, at Paris—had been published simultaneously in nine European languages and one Asiatic.

It is of interest to note, by the way, that the northeast passage around Europe and Asia—only just accomplished by Nordenskiöld — was prophesied over three hundred years ago by Gerard Mercator, distinguished by the cartographical projection which goes by his name. This famous old mathematician and geographer thought, also, that such an exploration would tend to open commercial routes between China and Western Europe. His exact words are—" The voyage to Cathaio [China] by the east is doubtless very easy, and I have oftentimes marvelled that, being so happily begun, it hath been left off, and the course changed into the west, after that more than half of the voyage was discovered." He also speaks of a great bay (being bordered by ice on two sides and land on the third, it might almost be styled a " bay ") beyond the island of Nova Zembla, into which " there fall great rivers, which passing through the whole country of Serica [modern China and Siberia,] and being, as I think, navigable with great vessels into the heart of the continent, may be an easy means whereby to traffic for all manner of merchandise, and transport them out of Cathaio, Mangi, Mien, and other kingdoms thereabouts, into England."

From Helsingfors one may go by steamer to Wiborg in twelve hours, or by rail, a distance of 195 miles, in about ten hours. Before leaving Stockholm I had decided upon the latter route of travel. The railway line passes through the most charming and picturesque region, a wooded country intersected by rivers and dotted with lakes. The interior of Finland is for the most part a vast plateau. Its entire area of 147,000 square miles is more abundantly supplied with lakes and swamps than any other part of the world, excepting possibly some districts of British America. Hence the origin of its name Fen-land, or swamp-land, or region of lakes, as some prefer to render it in English. The country of Holland has also its superficial character indicated in the etymology of its name, to wit, marsh-land. Fully one-half of Finland is covered with forests ; and the exports are accordingly chiefly timber and tar. Excellent post-roads, with regular rows of verst-poles (a verst is about two-thirds of an English mile), lead in every direction. Two-wheeled carrioles, similar to those used in Scandinavia, are also employed in Finland, and post-houses (dagbog and all) are conveniently situated and of a character to render this species of travelling quite as comfortable here as in Norway and Sweden. The interior of the country, however, is so intersected and broken up by the vast number of inland lakes which shoot out their winding arms and branches in every direction that, while offering the greatest facilities for internal navigation, they render land travelling very circuitous.

As in Scandinavia, the greater part of the population of Finland are peasants, who are accustomed to make their own clothes and furniture. They are affectionate, honest, hospitable, and peaceable, though in ancient times they were, according to Prichard, as savage as the Lapps. They were then divided into tribes which were generally at war with each other. The origin of the Finns, like that of the Lapps, has been a matter in great dispute among ethnologists, though if we are to accept the recently-expressed theory of an anonymous encyclopedia magnate, they came originally from Asia. "One of the least expected results of the decipherment of the Babylonian and Assyrian cruciform inscriptions is that the most ancient language found in this style of writing is strongly allied to the idioms of the Uralo-Finnic race, and that many of its words and the greater part of its grammatical forms particularly resemble the Finlandish. It is therefore conjectured that the Finnic race was in possession of the Tigris and Euphrates basin more than 4,000 years ago; and in retracing the ideographs of the cruciform to the objects they originally represented, it is found that the region where this system of writing was invented was a northern clime; at least one totally different from that of Babylonia and Assyria, destitute among other things, of large feline carnivora and of palm trees."

## CHAPTER XXII.

### Kalevala, the Great National Epic.

THE Helsingfors library contains a rich store of Finnish national sagas or tales and runes or songs. These are generally of a mythological character, though the folk-lore—what may be styled the literature of the ancient observances and customs, and also ideas, prejudices, and superstitions of the common people—is very largely represented. The value of these as illustrating remote periods of a nation's history, has been amply shown in Germany by the brothers Grimm. The songs are lyrical in form and are usually sung to the accompaniment of a species of harp with five strings. A collection of them was first made in 1835, by a native of Helsingfors named Elias Lönnrot. For years this poetical and patriotic enthusiast wandered from place to place in the most remote districts, living with the peasantry and taking down from their lips all that they knew of their popular songs. He thus eventually succeeded in collecting 23,000 verses, which he arranged as systematically as possible, and then published them under the title of Kalevala, the ancient name of Finland.

This great poem, which is justly regarded as a national epic, contains fifty runes or songs, written in eight-syllabled trochaic verse. Its story is briefly described as a struggle between the good and the bad powers of the universe, the subject of so many Oriental epics, with numerous episodes, and the introduction of mythology and magic. Speaking of the merits of this poem, Professor Max Müller, a most excellent authority, says: " From the mouths of the aged an epic poem has been collected, equalling the Iliad in length and completeness ; nay—if we can forget for a moment all that we in our youth learned to call beautiful—not less beautiful. A Finn is not a Greek, and a Wainaimoinen was not a Homer. But if a poet may take his colors from that nature by which he is surrounded ; if he may depict the men with whom he lives, Kalevala possesses merits not dissimilar from those of the Iliad, and will claim its place as the fifth national epic of the world, side by side with the Ionian songs, with the Mahàbárata, the Shanameh, and the Niebelunge."

The Kalevala has been translated into Swedish, French, German and Russian. A few specimens or selections have also been rendered into English. The general scope, style and metre of this great heroic poem have been imitated by our revered poet, Longfellow, in his unique American epic, the " Song of Hiawatha," the nearest approach to a real national epic that we have ever had. Longfellow is a great admirer of the Scandinavian literatures and when in Europe in 1836, he travelled extensively in these countries and acquainted himself with their languages. We have in both Kalevala and Hiawatha birch forests, roaring waters, and deep green lakes. Similar likewise are the heroic deeds, the moving adventures, and the quaint legends.

I cull a few specimen verses from the original of Kalevala. You will notice the frequent repetition of the same letter : this is owing largely to the fact that there are but nineteen letters in the Finnish alphabet.

> " Vaka vanha Wainaimoinen :
> Sen varsin valehtelitki,
> Ei sinna silloin nahty,
> Kan on meita kynnettihin,
> Meren kolkot kuokittihin,
> Kala-havat kaivettihin
> Kuuhutta kuletettaissa
> Aurinkoa autellaissa
> Otavoa ojennettaissa,
> Taivod tahitettaissa,
> Miekkojasi, mieliasi,
> Tauriasi, tuumiasi,
> . Waan kuitenki, kaikitenki
> Lahe en miekan mittelohon
> Sinun kanssasi katala,
> Kerallasi kehno rankka."

An idea of the matter and manner of this grand composition is furnished in a translation (as exact as the differences of genius and idiom in the two languages will permit) of a few verses of a song entitled " The Wooing."

> " The next morn the Maiden Aino,
> Sister fair of Youkahainen,
> Sought betimes the birchen forest
> Brooms to bind and twigs to gather,
> Choosing out the speckled birchwood ;

One to bring her father, binds she,
One a gift to bring her mother,
For her brother binds a third 'one.
　　Then by woodpath hastening homeward,
Flying from the forest darkness,
As she gains the bushy border,
Lo, before her Wainaimoinen,
Deftly spying out the maiden
In her trimly buckled bodice.
Thus the ancient bard addressed her:
　　' Wear not, lovely'maid, for others,
Only wear for me, O maiden.
Glossy pearls upon thy shoulders,
Shining cross upon thy bosom ;
Bind with silk for me thy tresses,
Plait for me thy braidlets golden.'
　　But the maiden quickly answered :
' Nevermore for thee or others
Will I all my life remaining
Deck my hair with silken ribbon,
Or with golden cross my bosom ;
Nay, I need no more the trinkets
Hither brought by ship or shallop ;
I will dress in humble raiment ;
All the food I ask a bread crust ;
With my father dwell forever,
In the cabin with my mother.' "

Hiawatha also indulges in the luxury of a " wooing,"
which I reproduce here that the reader may contrast
and compare the Finnish and the American poems.

　　" ' As unto the bow the cord is
So unto the man is woman,
Though she bends him, she obeys him,
Though she draws him, yet she follows,
Useless each without the other ! '
　　Thus the youthful Hiawatha
Said within himself and pondered,
Much perplexed by various feelings,

Listless, longing, hoping, fearing,
Dreaming still of Minnehaha,
Of the lovely Laughing Water,
In the land of the Dacotahs."

All persons intending to enter the public service of Finland must learn Finnish, which by imperial manifesto is to become the official language of the country after the year 1883. Until quite recently Swedish was the language of the upper classes. This accounts in part for the general poverty of the national literature. Heretofore it has been almost solely employed in works of a religious and moral character. The New Testament and Psalter was published in 1548, and the entire Bible in 1642. There are now publications in the native tongue on almost every branch of scientific research. These are, however, mainly translations or adaptations from the works of German or French scholars. An attempt has been made to translate Schiller and even Shakespeare into Finlandish, though with what success I did not learn. Two professors at the university of Helsingfors deliver their lectures in Finnish; and I understand that Professor Lönnrot of this university, the same who rescued from oblivion the fragmentary songs of the Kalevala, and now upwards of eighty years of age, has just published a valuable work on folk-lore entitled " A Collection of Ancient Finnish Popular Legends." Weekly Finlandish newspapers circulate among the peasantry, who welcome with avidity any addition to the limited stock of printed literature adapted to their intellectual capacity.

The Finns having succeeded so admirably with poetry, the reader will naturally wish to know whether they have not made progress in any other of the fine arts. Well, they have done something with the drama, more with music, but most with painting and sculpture. I shall not soon forget the very creditable display of the Finnish artists at the Paris International Exhibition of 1878. But I have not space here to do them justice, for my journey draws me onward to the end.

Wiborg I found to be the third city of Finland in point of population. It is situated at the end of a large bay where a review of the Russian Baltic fleet is generally held every summer. There is nothing in Wiborg calculated to especially interest strangers, who in fact, only visit it *en route* to the celebrated falls of Imatra, some forty miles distant to the north. These falls may be reached both by canal and post-road. It is best perhaps to go by one and return by the other. Every morning a small steamer leaves Wiborg for Lake Saima, "the thousand isles"—recalling, but not resembling, those in the St. Lawrence River. Lake Saima is nearly as large as Lake Wenern in Sweden. The Saima Canal is a grand triumph of engineering skill, being in some respects not unlike the Gotha Canal, to which I devoted a recent chapter. It was constructed at a cost of $2,000,000, by a Swedish engineer, in 1856. The lake is 256 feet above the Gulf of Finland, and it has therefore been found necessary to construct as many as twenty-eight locks to withstand so great a pressure of water as this difference in level naturally implies. These locks are most substantially built of the famous granite rock of Helsingfors. From a town on the lake we are forwarded by diligence to Imatra, where I find an immense but well-kept hotel.

The falls have been misnamed, since there is no perpendicular descent of water; they deserve rather to be designated as rapids. They vividly recalled those in the Niagara River below the suspension bridges. They are formed by the rushing of a small river between steep granite walls. The violence and roar of the water are appalling. The rapids gradually slope through a distance of about half a mile, the whole amount of descent being sixty feet. A capital view of them is obtained from the side of the river opposite the hotel. The style of transport thither is calculated, however, to try weak nerves and giddy heads, for you are drawn across the seething, tempestuous flood in a basket slung on wire ropes. The river must have been of much greater volume ages ago, for the limits of its old bed are clearly defined in the vicinity of the rapids. Here there are several pot-holes, containing boulders which cannot have gyrated for centuries.

The countries of Northwestern Europe are very rich in such interesting geological curiosities. In addition to those I have already described, there are on the southern coast of Norway, about 25 miles west of Christiania fiord, three giant caldrons which were discovered and dug out in 1873. They lie side by side, about 150 feet above the sea. The largest is 23 feet deep, 30 inches in diameter at the top, and five feet at the bottom. Though possibly produced in a different manner, the holes above mentioned are similar to those in the Glacier Garden at Lucerne, which are due to the action of water. This, flowing through the rifts in the glacier that ages past covered the rock, set in motion the stones beneath whereby the huge holes were hollowed out. The geological formation at Lucerne, if I remember aright, is sandstone. But potholes have been found in hard limestone and quartz, as at Soleure, at the foot of the Jura Mountains, where, on removing a mass of superincumbent sand and gravel to prepare for some quarrying operations, the rock beneath was found to be quite smooth and intersected with old water channels. The excavation being continued, a number of enormous basins, filled with great stones, were laid bare.

There is capital trout fishing above the " falls " of Imatra. Lake trout twenty pounds in weight have been taken from some of the pools. Graylings of two and three pounds' weight also abound. At a village in this vicinity on Lake Saima, there is a church to which, on a Sunday, come the Finns for miles around, the women often appearing in their gay national costumes. It is very amusing to watch these simple countryfolk going to or from the church in long, queer-shaped boats, which are rowed by about twenty women, while almost an equal number of men lounge and lazily smoke their pipes in the stern. In the Zuyder Zee of the Netherlands one may see many similar and quite as ridiculous interchanges of occupation between the sexes.

The return to Wiborg by carriole was over a good road and through a picturesque region. The following morning I took the train for St. Petersburg, and with its arrival, four hours later, in the capital city of all the Russias, my summer's wanderings through Denmark, Norway, Lapland, Sweden, and Finland were safely and happily completed.

And now, at the conclusion of my recital, whatever my defects of description may be, I can safely say that I have withstood the temptation which presents itself to every traveller, namely, that of giving a dramatic, not to say an unnaturally theatrical, tinge to personal experiences. To wander through countries and among nations that are new to one, is almost like stepping upon another planet and finding races akin, yet not akin, to the human family to which one belongs. To exaggerate the impressions thus made, to devise scenes, to create circumstances, and to weave together into artificial combinations events which actually occurred— these are the allurements which beset even the conscientious traveller when he begins to tell his tale. My claim is that I have resisted these temptations. It is not necessary to yield to them. The most prosaic mode of life acquires a little aureole of its own when we see it unfolding itself under conditions, and with environments, that to us are unfamiliar.

In the lands of the Far North much was new and strange to me. Their attractiveness was inherent in them and was not due to any charms loaned them by my imagination. If, therefore, I have failed to express that attractiveness in language proportioned to the effect it wrought in me, the suffering reader will not fail to recall that the author is alone to blame.

# INDEX.

## A.

THE END.